W9-CIL-471

M&M/MARS
SWEET TREAT COOKERY

Why Cook With M&M/MARS Products 3

Chocolate: The World's Favorite Flavor 3

The Choice Is Yours! 4

Ingredients Make The Difference 6

Storing Your Candy 7

Cooking Tips 7

Little Celebrations 8

Valentine Delights 20

Take A Cake And Make It Great 32

Easter 45

Elegant Desserts 59

Instant Desserts For Unexpected Guests 68

Do Ahead—Take From Freezer Or Refrigerator . 76

No-Trick Halloween Treats 85

Conversation Pieces 94

Top It Off 101

For Kids 105

Fun Christmas Food And Decorations 113

Creative Crafts 127

Index 149

The following are registered trademarks of MARS, Incorporated.

"M&M's" Plain Chocolate Candies   MARS Almond Bar
"M&M's" Peanut Chocolate Candies   SNICKERS Bar
MILKY WAY Bar   MARATHON Bar
3 MUSKETEERS Bar   MUNCH Peanut Bar
FOREVER YOURS Bar   STARBURST Fruit Chews
FUN SIZE Candies

ANOTHER BEST-SELLING COOKERY VOLUME FROM H.P. BOOKS

Publisher: Helen Fisher; Editor: Helen Fisher; Editor-in-Chief: Carl Shipman; Art Director: Don Burton; Book Design & Assembly: Laura Hardock, Tom Jakeway, Kathy Marie; Typography: Connie Brown, Cindy Coatsworth; Food Stylist: Mable Hoffman; Photography: George deGennaro Studios.

Published by H.P. Books, P.O. Box 5367, Tucson, AZ 85703   602/888-2150

ISBN: 0-89586-013-9
Library of Congress Catalog Card Number, 78-61008
© 1978 MARS, Inc.
Printed in U.S.A

Cover Photo: Orange Blossom Trifle, page 80.

Why Cook With M&M/MARS Products

The best reason for cooking with M&M/MARS products is their great taste. The tested recipes in this book capitalize on their delicious flavors in a variety of ways that make any meal a treat. But there are a lot of other reasons to use M&M/MARS products besides scrumptious taste.

Convenience—Every item is a packet of flavorful foods: chocolate, almonds, peanuts, caramel, nougat or chewy sugar crystals. You don't have to buy or prepare a lot of different ingredients to create delicious, unique desserts. In most cases it would be impossible for you to obtain the texture and flavor obtained from M&M/MARS products.

Pure Products—M&M/MARS products are made from the same fresh wholesome ingredients used in your own kitchen. When you cook with these products, you're cooking with Grade A milk, butter and honey; USDA graded #1 peanuts and almonds; USDA inspected egg whites; excellent cocoa and delicious chocolate.

Freshness—M&M/MARS products are enclosed in protective wrappers, keeping them both fresh and sanitary. Each package or wrapper has its own "Fresh Thru" date to guarantee freshness.

Kid Appeal—Children love treats you can whip up with familiar candy. Cakes, cookies and cupcakes can be easily garnished with M&M/MARS bars and candies; you needn't make decorations from scratch.

Chocolate: The World's Favorite Flavor

It doesn't seem possible that most of the world's people never tasted chocolate until the 19th century.

Chocolate originated in the New World. We know that in the 16th century Montezuma, powerful emperor of the Mexican Aztecs, drank a royal concoction called *chocolatl.* It was made by drying, roasting and grinding the dark brown cacao bean, which grew on trees in southern Mexican jungles. These beans were also used as currency: 10 beans could buy a rabbit, 4 could fetch a pumpkin.

The ground cacao bean made a semi-liquid paste. To it, Aztecs added vanilla, herbs and spices. Then they chilled this bitter brew with mountain snow. Supposedly, Montezuma drank enormous quantities of *chocolatl.* He doubtless offered the beverage to the conquering Spaniards, led by Cortes in 1519. Cortes recognized the commercial value of cacao beans. He brought them back to Spain and added sugar to the recipe. A continental craze began.

In France, England and Spain hot chocolate created a sensation among the aristocracy. It was an expensive drink, but soon, fashionable chocolate houses opened. None but the well-to-do could afford hot chocolate, which was mixed from hand-ground beans. But by 1730, the steam-driven chocolate grinder was invented and prices dropped.

Many more people could enjoy this fabulous New World flavor.

Chocolate, however, was not the pleasing, smooth-textured flavoring we know today. It wasn't until the 19th century that the quality of chocolate improved. This was the result of three important advances. The first was the invention of the cocoa press which could squeeze out part of the cocoa butter from ground beans. This made the remaining cocoa smoother and better tasting.

The second advance was the creation of *fondant* chocolate—velvety smooth, silky chocolate that was much more pleasant to eat than the gritty coarse variety chocolate lovers were accustomed to. It was made by running chocolate through a *conch*—a mixing machine shaped like a conch shell. In it, chocolate was heated and kneaded. This reduced the size of chocolate and sugar particles and produced a fine-textured chocolate.

The third advance was the invention of *milk chocolate* in 1876. An enterprising Swiss named Daniel Peter invented a way to mix the two flavors he loved: milk and chocolate. This produced a solid bar, rather than a liquid. Milk chocolate quickly became popular because its taste was light and smooth and most people still prefer it for eating.

The possibilities are endless. Upper level, from rear: Tangy Topped Cheesecake, page 48; Cream Puff Crown, 66; and Strawberry Cookie Tortes, 29. Lower level, left to right: Meringue Pears With Creamy Sauce, 18; Napoleans In-A-Hurry, 67; and Pineapple Upside-Down Cake, 35.

The Choice Is Yours!

M&M/MARS products are available in several flavors and styles, each a special treat.

"M&M's" Plain Chocolate Candies are milk chocolate coated with a colored sugar shell. Available in Singles, 1/2 lb., 3/4 lb. and 1 lb. packages.

"M&M's" Peanut Chocolate Candies contain tasty roasted peanuts surrounded by milk chocolate and coated with a colored sugar shell. The banner-yellow bag comes in the same Singles, 1/2 lb. and 1 lb. sizes as "M&M's" Plain Chocolate Candies.

MILKY WAY Bars start with a center of cocoa and malt-flavored nougat topped with caramel and coated with milk chocolate.

3 MUSKETEERS Bars take a cocoa vanilla-flavored nougat and coat it with milk chocolate.

FOREVER YOURS Bar is M&M/MARS only dark chocolate bar. Inside you will find a white nougat containing milk and natural vanilla flavor, topped with buttery-rich caramel, covered with rich Dark Chocolate.

MARS Almond Bars are honey-flavored nougat topped with almonds and covered with milk chocolate.

SNICKERS Bars contain a peanut-butter nougat layered with caramel and peanuts, and covered with milk chocolate.

MARATHON Bars are long bars of braided caramel covered with milk chocolate.

MUNCH Peanut Bars are made of peanuts embedded in a crackling brittle-like matrix.

STARBURST Fruit Chews are squares of chewy, tangy fruit flavors, designed for long-lasting flavor.

The Consumer Assurance of M&M/MARS Product Quality

Every candy product produced by M&M/MARS carries a written "Guarantee of Satisfaction" on the package label: "If this candy is not fresh and in good condition return unused portion for replacement. State where and when bought."

Candy labels carry an easily read freshness date and a code date of manufacture to help assure that fresh products reach the consumer.

M&M/MARS asks that its own associates act as quality conscious consumers of its products. Salespeople check freshness dates of candies wherever they are, and dispose of outdated products.

Every M&M/MARS product must meet a detailed set of product standards. Each bar must be uniform in such areas as moisture content, taste, size, color, weight and purity. Analysts regularly take samples from the production line to analyze and evaluate product quality.

Ingredients Make The Difference

M&M/MARS gets its fine ingredients from all over the world. Almonds come from California and peanuts from the southern United States, Africa and South America supply a variety of cocoa beans. Every ingredient entering an M&M/MARS candy plant is taste-tested and analyzed by testers and scientists employed by M&M/MARS. Finally, every M&M/MARS product is shipped quickly to ensure freshness and delicious flavor.

Chocolate

Simply defined, chocolate is prepared from cocoa beans that are roasted, shelled and ground. Dairy products are added to make *milk chocolate.*

The cocoa bean is harvested from the cocoa tree, *Theobroma cocoa,* which grows only in a narrow belt that girdles the globe, stretching 20 degrees north and 20 degrees south of the equator. MARS uses beans grown in Ghana, Nigeria, Ivory Coast, Cameroon and Brazil. Workers snip the pods from the trees, gather them in baskets, then split the pods with machetes to remove the beans. These beans are placed in leaf-lined boxes or in leaf-lined heaps on the ground to facilitate fermentation. During fermentation, the raw bitter taste disappears and flavor precursors typical of chocolate develop. When the beans are fermented, they change from white to a purplish brown color. Fermented beans are dried, cleaned, packed in burlap bags and shipped to chocolate manufacturers.

PROCESSING THE BEANS

Cocoa beans pick up odors easily, so they must be carefully stored away from items that can impart odors. Temperature and humidity are carefully controlled during storage to ensure freshness. The beans are cleaned prior to roasting by passing them through jets of air and over screens. Roasting the cleaned beans accomplishes two things. First, it brings the chocolate flavor to its peak. Second, the brittle outer shell can then be easily cracked and removed, which is called *winnowing.* This exposes the valuable part of the cocoa bean called the *nib.* The time and temperature of the roast depends on bean variety and the desired flavor. The nibs are conveyed to mills where they are ground and crushed to a rich-brown molten mass called *chocolate liquor.*

MAKING CHOCOLATE

To make today's fine chocolate, it is necessary to add extra cocoa butter to enhance the flavor, smooth the texture and make the liquor more fluid so that dry ingredients, like sugar, milk solids or flavors can be added. The mixture of ingredients is then refined by being passed through large rollers that reduce the size of the particles in the mixture. This is the step that develops flavor and enhances the eating properties of the product, so it is done carefully. Improperly refined chocolate tastes gritty. Properly refined chocolate is smooth and velvety.

Chocolate comes from the refiners in the form of flakes. To obtain the proper handling characteristics requires mechanical mixing and the addition of more cocoa butter. This mixing, called *conching,* was invented in the 19th century. Conching involves mixing the chocolate at high temperatures for several hours. Conching also drives off moisture, eliminates harsh flavors and develops the delicate flavors present in today's chocolate.

Caramel

A thick golden layer of buttery caramel is an important flavor ingredient in M&M/MARS SNICKERS Bars, MILKY WAY Bars, FOREVER YOURS Bars and MARATHON Bars. At the plant, confectioners blend corn syrup with sweetened condensed milk that contains creamery butter and flavoring agents. This mixture is cooked to a creamy yellow-brown color and cooled before being used in a candy bar.

Nougat

One of the best tastes to combine with chocolate is a fluffy, airy nougat such as those found in 3 MUSKETEERS Bar, MARS Almond Bar, SNICKERS Bar, MILKY WAY Bar and FOREVER YOURS Bar. M&M/MARS makes its nougats by beating egg whites and soy albumen into a mixture of cooked sugar and corn syrup. The mixture, referred to as *frappe,* is then super-whipped to give nougat its light texture.

SNICKERS Bar nougat has ground roasted peanuts added. MILKY WAY Bar nougat has cocoa, milk and malt added for smoothness and flavor.

3 MUSKETEERS Bar nougat has cocoa and vanilla added as flavors. FOREVER YOURS Bar nougat contains natural vanilla and milk. Pure clover Grade A honey is used to sweeten the nougat of MARS Almond Bar.

Peanuts

Whether drenched in milk chocolate for "M&M's" Peanut Chocolate Candies, layered into the smooth caramel of a SNICKERS Bar, or crowded into a MUNCH Peanut Bar, M&M/MARS still uses the finest grade peanuts that the South can grow. The raw peanuts are sorted, cleaned and tested to ensure that only the freshest mature peanuts are used. Whole peanuts are roasted to the full peanut flavor that is typical of "M&M's" Peanut Chocolate Candies. Peanuts for SNICKERS Bars are blanched to remove the outer skin, then roasted to a crispy-crunchy texture.

Almonds

Major ingredients in a MARS Almond Bar are the choice Mission and Drake varieties of almonds grown in California. After harvesting, the almonds are sorted, cleaned and shelled. Then they are roasted to provide a MARS Almond Bar with peak almond taste.

Storing Your Candy

M&M/MARS formulates its candies for maximum flavor at room temperature. To maintain texture, gloss and flavor, store candies at room temperature, below 80°F (25°C). Over 80°F (25°C), chocolate softens, loses its gloss, and the flavor and texture deteriorate faster. Always store chocolate candy in a dry place.

If you refrigerate or freeze MILKY WAY Bars, SNICKERS Bars and 3 MUSKETEERS Bars, they may last many months. Be sure to wrap the candy securely in plastic to prevent water condensation and to guard against odors from other foods. Chocolate may be frozen for 3 to 4 months with no change in flavor or texture.

Cooking Tips

Chocolate bars may be melted slowly in a heavy bottom saucepan, in a double boiler, or with a liquid such as water, milk or cream added. Use low heat to avoid scorching.

When melting without added ingredients, be sure all utensils are absolutely dry. Even small amounts of moisture can stiffen melting chocolate.

Only add liquids to chocolate if the chocolate is an ingredient in a recipe. Never add liquids to chocolate if you expect the chocolate to harden again.

If you want to melt chocolate bars in a microwave, place the candy with liquid in a glass container in the microwave and set it on FULL POWER for 90 seconds. Stir and then heat again with microwave on FULL POWER for 30 seconds.

Handle chocolate as little as possible. Too much handling can dull the gloss and harm the texture.

Two FUN SIZE Candies can be substituted for one regular-size candy bar in the recipes in this book.

Little Celebrations

What do you do on a day that is just another day? Make it a special celebration with one of these easy desserts. Unbirthdays are ideal occasions, but so are unanniversaries or any un-holiday. A good report card or any special achievement is worth celebrating. Try Super Easy Apple Turnovers, page 10, or Super Trio Cookies, page 12. Or, take a traditional favorite and make it better with Chocolate Cherry Pie, page 15.

Baked Chocolate Alaskas

Each guest has his own spectacular meringue-covered dessert.

1 (10-3/4 oz.) pound cake
8 FUN SIZE Candies—MILKY WAY,
   SNICKERS or 3 MUSKETEERS Bars
2 egg whites
1/8 teaspoon cream of tartar

1/8 teaspoon salt
1/4 cup sugar
1/2 teaspoon vanilla extract
Ice cream, if desired

Preheat oven to 350°F (175°C). Trim crusts from pound cake, if desired. Cut crosswise into 8 even slices. Place slices on a baking sheet. Center a candy bar on each slice. Beat egg whites, cream of tartar and salt until egg whites form soft peaks when beater is lifted. Gradually add sugar 1 table-spoon at a time, beating constantly. Add vanilla and continue beating until mixture is stiff and glossy. Spread meringue on top and sides of candy. Seal to edges of cake. Bake 12 to 15 minutes or until meringue is lightly browned. Serve with ice cream, if desired. Makes 8 servings.

Confetti Cream Cones

This lovely idea comes from Scandinavia.

1/4 cup butter or margarine
1/4 cup sugar
2/3 cup flour
2 egg whites, stiffly beaten

Peanut Confetti Filling, see below
"M&M's" Peanut Chocolate Candies,
   for garnish

Peanut Confetti Filling:
1 (3-oz.) pkg. vanilla-flavored
   pudding and pie filling (not instant)
1-1/2 cups milk
2 egg yolks beaten

1 (4-1/2-oz.) container frozen whipped
   topping, thawed
1 teaspoon vanilla extract
1/2 cup "M&M's" Peanut Chocolate Candies

Preheat oven to 425°F (220°C). In a small bowl, cream butter or margarine and sugar until light and fluffy. Stir in flour. Fold in beaten egg whites. Drop 2 rounded teaspoonfuls of dough 4 inches apart on an ungreased baking sheet. Spread each to a 5-inch circle with spatula. Bake 5 minutes or until edges begin to color. Quickly remove cookies from baking sheet. Fold into cone shapes. Place points down in soft drink bottles or narrow glasses until cone shape is set. Repeat to make 12 cones. If cookies become too brittle, return to oven to soften. Prepare Peanut Confetti Filling. Fill cones with filling and candy mixture. Garnish with additional candies. Store in refrigerator. Makes 6 servings.

Peanut Confetti Filling:
Prepare pudding following package directions using 1-1/2 cups milk. Remove pan from heat. Beat 1/2 cup hot pudding mixture into beaten egg yolks. Stir yolk mixture gradually into remaining pudding. Cook and stir 1 minute. Cool completely. Beat pudding until smooth. Fold in thawed topping and vanilla. Chill. Before serving, fold in candies.

Today's Bread Pudding

An old-fashioned dessert that tastes even better with chocolate.

1-1/2 cups "M&M's" Plain Chocolate Candies
3 cups milk
3 eggs
1 teaspoon salt
1 teaspoon ground cinnamon

2 teaspoons vanilla extract
10 slices day-old bread,
   cubed or torn into small pieces
1/2 cup raisins

Preheat oven to 325°F (165°C). In a medium saucepan, combine candies and 1 cup of the milk. Melt over low heat, stirring until smooth. Cool slightly. In a medium mixing bowl, beat remaining 2 cups milk, eggs, salt, cinnamon and vanilla. Add chocolate mixture. Toss bread cubes and raisins together in a 2-quart round glass baking dish. Pour chocolate-milk mixture over all. Bake 60 to 70 minutes or until knife inserted near center comes out clean. Serve warm or cold with cream. Makes 8 servings.

Super-Easy Apple Turnovers

Super easy, super tasting.

1 (11-oz.) pkg. pie crust mix
2 tablespoons sugar
8 FUN SIZE Candies—MARATHON Bars

1/2 (20-oz.) can sliced apples, well drained
3 tablespoons apricot preserves

Preheat oven to 375°F (190°C). Prepare pie crust mix according to package directions, adding sugar to dry mix. Roll out on lightly floured surface into 20" x 10" rectangle. Cut into eight 5-inch squares. Center candy bar on one half of each square. Arrange 3 apple slices on top of each candy bar. Spoon about 1 teaspoon preserves over apples on each pastry square. Moisten edges of pastry with water. Fold in half. Press edges together with fork. Make 2 or 3 slits in top of each turnover. Bake 20 minutes or until golden brown. Serve warm. Makes 8 turnovers.

How To Make Super-Easy Apple Turnovers

1/Place candy bar on one half of pie crust squares. Top bar with apple slices and spoon about 1 teaspoon apricot preserves over apples.

2/Moisten edges of pastry with water. Fold dough over candy, apples and preserves. With fork tines, press edges together to seal.

Peanut-Caramel Apple Tart

A classic upside-down fruit tart with an innovative topping.

2 MARATHON Bars, cut up
1/3 cup apricot preserves
3 to 4 medium Golden Delicious apples, peeled, cored
1 tablespoon flour

1/2 teaspoon cinnamon
1/2 teaspoon nutmeg
1/2 (11-oz.) pkg. pie crust mix (not sticks)
2 tablespoons sugar
1 MUNCH Peanut Bar, chopped

Preheat oven to 425°F (220° C). In a small saucepan, combine MARATHON Bars and apricot preserves. Stir over low heat until candy melts. Spread in bottom of a 9-inch, round cake pan. Slice apples about 1/4 inch thick. Beginning in the center, arrange apple slices in overlapping circles in pan. Combine flour, cinnamon and nutmeg; sprinkle over apples. Combine pie crust mix and sugar; mix according to package directions. Roll dough into a 9-inch circle. Place over apples in pan. Press down lightly. Bake 25 minutes or until pastry is brown and sauce is bubbly. Let stand in pan 15 minutes. Invert onto serving plate. Sprinkle with peanut candy. Serve warm or at room temperature. Makes 6 to 8 servings.

Crumb Cupcakes

Sugar and spice plus chocolate are nice.

3/4 cup milk
1 tablespoon vinegar
2 3 MUSKETEERS Bars, cut up
2 teaspoons water
2 cups flour
1 cup sugar
3/4 cup butter or margarine

1/2 cup raisins
1/2 cup chopped walnuts
1 teaspoon ground cinnamon
1 teaspoon ground nutmeg
1 teaspoon baking soda
1 egg

Preheat oven to 350°F (175°C). Line 18 muffin cups with paper liners. In a small bowl, mix milk and vinegar. In a small saucepan, combine candy and water. Melt over low heat, stirring until smooth. Remove from heat and stir in milk mixture. In a large bowl, mix flour and sugar. Cut in butter or margarine until mixture resembles fine crumbs. Reserve 1 cup crumbs. Stir raisins, chopped walnuts, cinnamon, nutmeg and baking soda into remaining crumbs. Add egg and chocolate mixture. Beat thoroughly. Fill each muffin cup slightly less than half full. Sprinkle each cupcake with reserved crumbs. Bake 20 to 25 minutes. Makes 18 cupcakes.

Party Perfect Bars

Easy-to-make bar cookies are the star of the day.

1-1/4 cups flour	2 eggs
1/4 teaspoon baking soda	1 teaspoon vanilla extract
1/4 teaspoon salt	1 (12-oz.) pkg. "M & M's" Plain Chocolate
1/2 cup butter or margarine	Candies, chopped
1/3 cup granulated sugar	1/2 cup chopped pecans
1/3 cup brown sugar, firmly packed	

Preheat oven to 350°F (175°C). Grease a 9" x 9" baking pan. In a small bowl, stir together flour, baking soda and salt. In a medium bowl, cream butter or margarine, granulated and brown sugars. Add eggs and vanilla. Beat until light and fluffy. Stir flour mixture into creamed mixture. Add chopped candies and nuts. Spread in prepared baking pan. Bake 40 minutes. Cut into 2-inch squares. Makes about 16 bars.

Super Trio Cookies

Make this your cookie jar staple.

1 (16-oz.) pkg. "M&M's" Plain Chocolate Candies	3/4 cup granulated sugar
2-1/2 cups flour	3/4 cup light brown sugar, firmly packed
1/2 teaspoon baking soda	2 eggs
1/2 teaspoon salt	1 teaspoon vanilla extract
1 cup butter or margarine	1 cup chopped pecans

Preheat oven to 350°F (175° C). Grease baking sheets. Coarsely chop about 1-1/2 cups of the candies; reserve remaining whole candies for decoration. Stir together flour, baking soda and salt. In a large bowl, cream butter or margarine, granulated sugar and brown sugar. Add eggs and vanilla. Beat until light and fluffy. Add flour mixture gradually. Add chopped candies and pecans. Drop batter by rounded tablespoonfuls onto prepared baking sheets. Bake 6 to 7 minutes. Remove from oven. Put 3 whole candies on top of each cookie. Return to oven and bake 3 to 5 minutes longer or until light brown. Remove from baking sheets. Cool on wire rack. Some candies will crack in baking, adding texture to the cookies. Makes about 60 cookies.

For a great cold treat: Fold chopped MARS Almond, SNICKERS, MILKY WAY, FOREVER YOURS or 3 MUSKETEERS Bars into slightly softened ice cream and freeze until firm.

Clockwise from top: Party Perfect Bars, Super Trio Cookies and Oat & Nut Squares, page 14.

Oat & Nut Squares   **Photo on page 13.**

Quick to make with convenience products.

1 (18-oz.) pkg. oatmeal cookie mix
6 MARATHON Bars, cut up
2/3 cup evaporated milk

1 cup chopped nuts
1 teaspoon vanilla extract

Preheat oven to 350°F (175°C). Grease a 13" x 9" baking pan. Prepare cookie mix according to package directions. Spread in baking pan. In a small saucepan, combine candy and evaporated milk. Melt over low heat, stirring until smooth. Add nuts and vanilla. Spread over oatmeal mixture. Bake 35 to 40 minutes. Cut into 2-inch squares. Makes about 24 squares.

Banana Bars

A great hit anytime.

3 MARS Almond Bars, cut up
1/4 cup milk
1 (15-oz.) pkg. banana quick bread mix
1 egg

1/4 cup oil
1 banana, mashed
Powdered sugar

Preheat oven to 350°F (175°C). Grease a 9" x 9" baking pan. In a small saucepan, combine candy and milk. Melt over low heat, stirring until smooth. In a medium bowl, combine melted candy, bread mix, egg, oil and banana. Mix just until blended. Spread into prepared baking pan. Bake 25 to 30 minutes or until done. Cool; sprinkle with powdered sugar. Cut into 3" x 1-1/2" bars. Makes about 27 bars.

Banana Chocolate Floats

Try this dessert on a hot summer night.

1/2 cup "M & M's" Plain Chocolate Candies
1/2 cup hot milk
1-1/2 cups cold milk
2 medium bananas, cut in chunks

1 teaspoon vanilla extract
1 cup vanilla ice cream (1/2 pint)
Banana slices for garnish

Place candies in a blender container. Add hot milk. Cover container and blend until smooth. Add cold milk, banana chunks and vanilla extract. Cover and blend until smooth. Spoon equal amounts of ice cream into chilled glasses. Pour chocolate mixture over ice cream. Garnish with banana slices. Makes 4 servings.

Chocolate Cherry Pie

Add flair to a celebration.

1 (21-oz.) can cherry pie filling
4 **FOREVER YOURS** Bars, chopped

1 tablespoon lemon juice
1 (9-in.) unbaked pie shell

Preheat oven to 425°F (220°C). Combine pie filling, candy and lemon juice. Spread in pie shell. Bake 12 to 15 minutes or until pie shell is golden brown. Makes 6 to 8 servings.

How To Make Chocolate Cherry Pie

1/Combine chopped candy bars with lemon juice and stir into cherry pie filling.

2/Spread cherry filling mixture evenly into prepared pie shell and bake.

Caramel-Banana Cream Pie

Here's a pie easy enough to make for unexpected company.

3 MARATHON Bars
2 tablespoons milk
1 (3-5/8-oz.) pkg. vanilla pudding and
   pie filling mix
1-1/2 cups milk

1/2 cup whipping cream, whipped
2 bananas
2 tablespoons lemon juice
1 (9-in.) graham cracker crust, baked

In a small saucepan, combine candy and 2 tablespoons milk. Melt over low heat, stirring until smooth. Prepare pudding according to package directions, using only 1-1/2 cups milk. Cool slightly. Divide pudding into 2 small bowls. Stir candy mixture into half the pudding. Fold whipped cream into remaining half. Slice bananas into a small bowl. Sprinkle with lemon juice and toss lightly. Place 1/3 bananas on bottom of pie crust. Spoon chocolate filling over bananas. Place second 1/3 of the bananas on top. Spoon vanilla filling over bananas. Garnish with remaining bananas. Refrigerate until ready to serve. Makes 6 to 8 servings.

Variation

Banana pudding can be substituted for vanilla pudding.

Pumpkin Ice Cream Pie

This will become a holiday tradition at your house.

Crust, see below
1 cup cooked or canned pumpkin
1/2 cup brown sugar, firmly packed
1 teaspoon ground cinnamon

1/4 teaspoon ground nutmeg
1/8 teaspoon ground cloves
1/4 teaspoon salt
1 qt. vanilla ice cream, softened

Crust:

4 MUNCH Peanut Bars, ground
1 cup graham cracker crumbs

1/4 cup butter or margarine, melted

Prepare crust. In a medium bowl, combine pumpkin with sugar, cinnamon, nutmeg, cloves and salt. Stir in ice cream, spoon into cooled crust. Cover with foil or plastic wrap and freeze. Allow pie to stand in refrigerator 30 to 40 minutes before serving. Makes 6 to 8 servings.

Crust:

Preheat oven to 350° F (175°C). In a medium bowl, combine candy, graham cracker crumbs and melted butter or margarine. Press into a 9-inch glass pie dish. Bake 8 minutes. Remove from oven and cool on wire rack.

Meringue Pears

Something really special!

2 cups sugar
2 cups water
1/2 lemon, thinly sliced
6 whole ripe pears with stems, peeled
1 teaspoon vanilla extract

Meringue, see below
Additional sugar
1-1/2 cups Creamy Chocolate Sauce,
   page 102

Meringue:
3 egg whites
1/8 teaspoon cream of tartar

1/8 teaspoon salt
1/2 cup sugar

In a medium saucepan, combine sugar, water and sliced lemon. Heat to boiling. Add pears. Reduce heat and simmer uncovered 10 to 15 minutes. Turn pears several times. Cook until tender. Add vanilla. Chill in syrup. Arrange chilled pears in a large shallow baking dish, leaving space between them. Preheat oven to 325°F (165°C). Prepare meringue. Spread meringue over top 3/4 of pears, leaving stems uncovered. Or, press meringue through pastry bag with star tip. Sprinkle meringues with additional sugar. Bake 10 to 12 minutes until meringue is light brown. For each dessert, spoon about 1/4 cup Creamy Chocolate Sauce into shallow dish. Place meringue pear in sauce. Pears may be served warm or chilled. Makes 6 servings.

Meringue:
Beat egg whites until foamy. Add cream of tartar and salt. Beat until egg whites form soft peaks. Add sugar 1 tablespoon at a time. Beat until stiff and glossy.

Buttery Flower Cookies

Welcome sweet springtime with decorated flower shapes.

2-1/2 cups flour
1/2 teaspoon baking powder
1/4 teaspoon salt
1 cup butter or margarine
3/4 cup sugar

1 egg
1 teaspoon vanilla extract
1/2 teaspoon almond extract
About 1/4 cup "M&M's" Plain Chocolate
   Candies

Preheat oven to 400°F (205°C). In a medium bowl, combine flour, baking powder and salt. In a large bowl, cream butter or margarine and sugar. Add egg, vanilla and almond extract. Beat until light and fluffy. Stir in flour mixture. Force dough through cookie press onto ungreased baking sheet. Decorate with candies, as desired. Bake 5 to 7 minutes until golden brown. Makes about 60 cookies.

Oatmeal Cookies

Perfect for the first day of school.

3/4 cup shortening
3/4 cup brown sugar, firmly packed
1/2 cup granulated sugar
2 eggs
1 teaspoon vanilla extract
3 cups oats

1 cup flour
1 teaspoon salt
1/2 teaspoon baking soda
3 MUNCH Peanut Bars, crushed
1 cup raisins, if desired

Preheat oven to 350°F (175°C). Grease cookie sheets. In a large bowl, cream together shortening, brown and granulated sugars. Add eggs and vanilla. Beat until light and fluffy. Combine oats, flour, salt and baking soda. Beat into creamed mixture. Stir in crushed candy and raisins, if desired. Drop by heaping teaspoonfuls 1 inch apart on prepared cookie sheets. Bake 15 minutes or until cookies are golden brown. Remove cookies from oven and let cool slightly on baking sheets. Remove and let cool on wire racks. Makes 48 to 60 cookies.

Hot Caramel Pecan Rolls

Good enough for company brunch, easy enough for everyday breakfast.

2 MARATHON Bars, cut up
1/4 cup water
2 tablespoons butter or margarine

1/4 cup chopped pecans
1 (10-oz.) pkg. refrigerated biscuits

Preheat oven to 350°F (175°C). Butter an 8-inch square pan. In a small saucepan, combine candy, water and butter or margarine. Melt over low heat, stirring until smooth. Pour 1/2 of the candy mixture into prepared pan. Sprinkle with pecans. Cut biscuits in half crosswise and arrange in rows over candy mixture in pan. Drizzle remaining candy mixture over biscuits. Bake 20 minutes or until light brown. Turn out immediately. Spread any candy mixture remaining in pan over rolls. Serve warm. Makes 5 to 6 servings.

To ensure melting without burning, stir the chocolate constantly over low heat or in a double boiler over hot water.

Valentine Delights

The sweetest holiday of the year can be made even better. Try Meringue Hearts With Chocolate Mousse, page 30, or Strawberry Crunch Shortcake, page 23. Or start any day with Sticky Buns, page 24. You'll love them.

Ice Cream Crepes With Almond Sauce

Prepare this lovely dish for your special valentine. Freeze extra crepes for another day.

2 eggs
1/2 cup flour
1 tablespoon sugar
1/2 cup milk
2 tablespoons water

2 teaspoons butter, melted
Chocolate Almond Sauce, page 102
1 pint brick strawberry or peppermint
   ice cream
1 tablespoon butter or margarine, if desired

In a medium bowl, beat eggs. Gradually add flour and sugar alternately with milk and water. Beat with electric mixer or whisk until smooth. Beat in butter. Refrigerate batter 1 hour before making crepes. Prepare Chocolate Almond Sauce and keep warm. Cut ice cream lengthwise into four equal sticks. Cut each stick in half. Place in freezer. Melt a small amount of butter in a small skillet. Place skillet on medium-high heat. Pour 2 to 3 tablespoons of batter into skillet with one hand while lifting the skillet above the heat with the other. Tilt skillet in all directions, swirling the batter so it covers the bottom of the pan in a very thin layer. Return to heat and cook until bottom of crepe is browned. Turn carefully with spatula and brown other side for a few seconds. Remove from skillet and stack on plate. Place a stick of ice cream on each crepe and fold two sides over, making a roll. Place on dessert plates. Serve at once with warm Chocolate Almond Sauce. Makes 8 crepes.

Macaroon Nougats

Chocolate coconut drops that melt in your mouth.

1 (7.2-oz.) pkg. fluffy white frosting mix
1/3 cup sifted powdered sugar
1/2 teaspoon salt

1/3 cup boiling water
4 3 MUSKETEERS Bars, chopped
1 (4-oz.) pkg. shredded coconut

Preheat oven to 300°F (150°C). Line 2 baking sheets with parchment or brown paper. In a deep narrow bowl, combine frosting mix, powdered sugar and salt. Add boiling water. Beat on highest speed with electric mixer until stiff peaks form, about 5 minutes. Fold in chopped candy and coconut. Drop by rounded teaspoonfuls on baking sheets. Bake 30 minutes or until light brown. Remove at once from paper and cool completely on wire rack. Makes about 36 nougats.

Calypso Chocolate

Rich, warm and tropical.

1/2 cup "M&M's" Plain Chocolate Candies
1 teaspoon instant coffee
1/8 teaspoon ground cinnamon
1 (3" x 1") strip orange peel

2 cups hot milk
Whipped cream
Long orange peel strips, for garnish

Place candies, coffee, cinnamon and 3" x 1" strip of orange peel in a blender container. Add hot milk. Cover container and blend until smooth. Pour into warm glasses or mugs. Top with whipped cream. Garnish with orange strips. Makes about 2-1/4 cups, or 3 or 4 servings.

Something Special Fondue

The easiest, tastiest chocolate fondue fun.

About 2 cups half-and-half
12 MILKY WAY Bars, cut up

1 pint strawberries
Pound cake

In a medium saucepan, combine 1-1/2 cups half-and-half and candy. Melt over low heat, stirring until smooth. Add more half-and-half as needed to maintain fondue consistency. Remove from heat. Pour into fondue pot. Keep warm with low flame. Wash strawberries, hull if desired. Cut cake into 1/2-inch slices. Cut slices into 1-inch cubes or into heart shapes with a 1-inch heart-shaped cookie cutter. Use strawberries and cake pieces for dipping. Makes 3 cups fondue.

Variations
Fresh pineapple, banana, pears or apples can be used for dippers.

Strawberry Crunch Shortcake

Spectacular!

2-1/3 cups biscuit mix
3 MUNCH Peanut Bars, crushed
1 cup (1/2 pint) dairy sour cream

1/3 to 1/2 cup milk
Strawberry Filling, see below

Strawberry Filling:
2 pints fresh strawberries
1/2 cup sugar
2 (3-oz.) pkgs. cream cheese, softened

1 teaspoon vanilla extract
1 cup whipping cream

Preheat oven to 425°F (220°C). In a medium bowl, combine biscuit mix and 2/3 of the crushed candy. Reserve remaining candy for garnish. Cut in sour cream with pastry blender or 2 knives. Stir in enough milk to make a soft dough. Spread in 2 ungreased 8-inch, round cake pans. Bake about 20 minutes or until golden brown. Cool. Place 1 layer on a serving platter. Prepare Strawberry Filling. Spread half the cream cheese mixture on bottom layer. Spoon on half the sliced strawberries. Place second layer over strawberries. Spread remaining cream cheese mixture on top. Outline outer edge of cake with reserved half strawberries. Sprinkle with reserved crushed candy. Serve warm or chilled. Makes 6 servings.

Strawberry Filling:
Wash and hull strawberries. Reserve 12 pretty strawberries for decoration. If large, slice in half; set aside. Slice remaining strawberries and sprinkle with 1/4 cup sugar. Set aside. In a medium bowl, beat cream cheese until smooth. Add remaining 1/4 cup sugar, vanilla and whipping cream. Beat until thickened. The filling will be soft.

Variation
Substitute 2 (10-oz.) pkgs. frozen strawberries or fresh, frozen or canned peach slices for the fresh strawberries.

Ice Cream Nog

Fun new drinks from the blender.

1/2 cup "M&M's" Plain Chocolate Candies
1/2 cup hot milk
1/2 cup cold milk

1 cup vanilla ice cream (1/2 pint)
2 scoops vanilla ice cream

Place candy in a blender container. Add hot milk. Cover container and blend until smooth. Add cold milk and 1 cup ice cream. Blend until smooth. Pour into glasses. Top each with a scoop of ice cream. Makes 2 servings.

Variations

Quick Chocolate Malted Nog: Blend 2 tablespoons malted milk powder with candy and milk.
Quick Chocolate-Coffee Nog: Blend 2 tablespoons instant coffee with candy and milk.
Quick Chocolate Peppermint Nog: Substitute peppermint ice cream for vanilla ice cream.

Strawberry Parfaits With Chocolate Sauce

Ice cream sundae deluxe.

Tiny Cookie Hearts, see below
1 cup "M&M's" Plain Chocolate Candies
1/4 cup half-and-half
1/4 cup light corn syrup
1/8 teaspoon cream of tartar

3 to 4 tablespoons half-and-half
1 cup "M&M's" Peanut Chocolate Candies, chopped
1 qt. strawberry ice cream, slightly softened

Tiny Cookie Hearts:
1 (18-oz.) pkg. refrigerated sugar cookie dough

Prepare Tiny Cookie Hearts. In a small saucepan combine plain candies, 1/4 cup half-and-half, corn syrup and cream of tartar. Melt over low heat, stirring until smooth. Chill. Add 3 to 4 tablespoons half-and-half to thin sauce to desired consistency. Spoon half the chopped peanut candies into 6 chilled parfait glasses. Spoon about half the ice cream into glasses. Repeat with remaining chopped candies and ice cream. Garnish with Tiny Cookie Hearts. Serve with the chocolate sauce. Makes 6 servings.

Tiny Cookie Hearts:
Preheat oven to 350°F (175°C). Slice refrigerated sugar cookie dough 1/4 inch thick. Cut each slice into quarters. Cut a small wedge out of rounded side of each and round edge to make heart shape. Place on ungreased baking sheet. Bake 7 minutes or until lightly browned. Let stand on baking sheet 1 minute. Remove and cool on wire rack.

Sticky Buns

Start the day with something special.

1 (13.75-oz.) pkg. hot roll mix
4 SNICKERS Bars
2 tablespoons milk

4 tablespoons butter or margarine, melted
1/2 cup brown sugar, firmly packed
1/2 teaspoon ground cinnamon

Prepare hot roll mix according to package directions. In a small saucepan, combine candy and milk. Melt over low heat, stirring until smooth. Coat bottom of a 9-inch, round cake pan with 2 tablespoons of the butter or margarine. Pour melted candy into cake pan. On a lightly floured surface, roll out dough to a 12" x 7" rectangle. Brush dough with remaining 2 tablespoons butter. In a small bowl, combine brown sugar and cinnamon. Sprinkle over dough. Starting with the 12-inch edge, roll up jelly-roll fashion. Slice into 12 sections. Arrange cut side up on melted candy. Cover and let rise in warm place until doubled in bulk, about 25 minutes. Preheat oven to 375°F (190°C). Bake 20 to 25 minutes or until golden brown. Invert pan immediately onto serving plate. Lift pan and spoon any remaining glaze in pan over the rolls. Cool slightly. Serve warm or cool. Makes 12 rolls.

Chocolate-Streusel Topped Coffeecake

Perfect quick-mix coffeecake for Sunday morning brunch.

Streusel Topping, see below
2-1/2 cups biscuit mix
3 tablespoons sugar

1/2 teaspoon ground cinnamon
2 eggs
2/3 cup milk

Streusel Topping:
1/3 cup biscuit mix
2 tablespoons brown sugar, firmly packed
2 tablespoons butter or margarine

1 cup chopped "M&M's"
Plain Chocolate Candies

Preheat oven to 375°F (190°C). Grease a 9-inch square baking pan. Prepare Streusel Topping. Set aside. In a medium bowl, stir together biscuit mix, sugar and cinnamon. Add eggs and milk. Beat with a spoon just until smooth, about 30 seconds. Pour into prepared pan. Sprinkle with Streusel Topping. Bake 25 to 30 minutes or until wooden pick inserted near center comes out dry. Makes 6 to 9 servings.

Streusel Topping:
In a small bowl, stir together biscuit mix and brown sugar. Cut in butter or margarine to form coarse crumbs. Stir in chopped candies.

How To Make
Chocolate-Streusel Topped Coffeecake

1/Stir chopped plain candies into biscuit mix and brown sugar. Cut in 2 tablespoons butter until mixture resembles coarse crumbs.

2/Pour coffeecake batter into prepared pan. Drop Chocolate Streusel topping from teaspoon or sprinkle onto batter and bake.

Valentine Meringue

For your sweetheart.

1 (7.2-oz). pkg. fluffy white frosting mix
1/3 cup sifted powdered sugar
1/2 cup boiling water

2 SNICKERS Bars, finely chopped
1 qt. strawberry or peppermint ice cream
Chocolate Almond Sauce, page 102

Preheat oven to 275°F (135°C). Line a baking sheet with aluminum foil or heavy brown paper. Draw a heart about 10" x 10" on foil or paper. In a small narrow bowl, combine frosting mix and powdered sugar. Add boiling water. Beat at highest speed with electric mixer until stiff and glossy, 3 to 5 minutes. Fold in chopped candy. Using pastry tube and large tip or spoon edge, make a 1-inch wide heart shape on foil or paper. Spread remaining meringue mixture in center of heart with a spatula. Bake 2 hours. Remove from oven. Cool 10 minutes. Peel off paper or foil. Cool completely on wire rack. Fill with ice cream. Put in freezer until ready to serve. Serve with Chocolate Almond Sauce. Makes 6 servings.

Chocolate Cheesecake Cups

Two-tone dessert for your next Valentine party.

18 to 20 shortbread cookies
1 tablespoon butter or margarine, melted
4 MILKY WAY BARS, cut up
2 tablespoons water
1/2 teaspoon brandy extract
1/4 cup sugar
1 tablespoon unflavored gelatin (1 envelope)
1/4 teaspoon salt

1 cup milk
2 eggs, separated
1 (8-oz.) pkg. cream cheese,
  room temperature
1 tablespoon lemon juice
1 teaspoon vanilla extract
1 cup (1/2 pint) dairy sour cream
1/4 cup sugar

Line 18 muffin cups with 2-1/2-inch fluted baking cups. Crush cookies to make fine crumbs. In a small bowl, combine 1 cup crumbs and melted butter or margarine. Spoon equal amounts of crumb mixture into fluted baking cups. Press down lightly. Chill. In a small saucepan combine candy and water. Melt over low heat, stirring until smooth. Add brandy extract. Cool to room temperature, stirring several times, but do not allow to set. In a medium saucepan, combine 1/4 cup sugar, gelatin and salt. Beat in milk and egg yolks. Cook over low heat, stirring constantly, until mixture coats spoon. Cool 15 minutes. In a medium bowl, beat cream cheese until smooth. Slowly beat in custard mixture. Stir in lemon juice and vanilla. Chill until mixture begins to set. Add sour cream. Mix well. In a small bowl, beat egg whites until soft peaks form when beater is lifted. Gradually beat in 1/4 cup sugar. Continue beating until stiff and glossy. Fold into cream cheese mixture. Remove 2 cups cheese mixture. Carefully fold chocolate mixture into remaining cheese mixture. Spoon equal amounts of chocolate mixture into prepared cups and top each with reserved cheese mixture. Refrigerate until ready to serve. Makes 18 servings.

Variation

Marbled Cheesecake Cups: Spoon both mixtures alternately into prepared cups.

Double-Decker Heart Cookies

A double chocolate-filled treat.

3 cups flour
1 teaspoon baking powder
1/2 teaspoon salt
1 cup butter or margarine
1 cup light brown sugar, firmly packed
1 egg

2 tablespoons half-and-half
1 tablespoon lemon juice
6 SNICKERS Bars
Powdered sugar, if desired
Ready-to-spread frosting, if desired

Preheat oven to 325°F (165°C). Stir together flour, baking powder and salt. In a mixing bowl, beat butter or margarine until light. Add brown sugar. Beat until light and fluffy. Beat in egg. Add flour mixture alternately with half-and-half and lemon juice. Wrap dough in wax paper and chill. On a lightly floured surface, roll out 1/2 at a time to 1/8-inch thickness. Cut with a 2-1/2-inch heart-shaped cookie cutter. Place on ungreased baking sheet. Bake 10 minutes or until edges are light brown. Let stand on baking sheet 1 minute. Remove and cool on wire rack. Cut each candy bar into 12 slices. Place 2 slices on half of the cookies and top with a second cookie. Arrange cookies on baking sheet. Heat in 325°F (165°C) oven to soften candy, about 5 minutes. Gently press cookies together while hot. Cool. Sprinkle with powdered sugar or pipe frosting through pastry tip around edges of cookies, as desired. Makes 36 filled cookies.

Special Coeur à la Crème

A rich chocolate-cheese dessert traditionally made in a heart-shaped mold.

6 MILKY WAY Bars, cut up
1/4 cup milk
1 cup (8-oz.) cottage cheese
1 (8-oz.) pkg. cream cheese, softened

1/2 teaspoon almond extract
1 cup whipping cream, whipped
Fresh strawberries

In a small saucepan, combine candy and milk. Melt over low heat, stirring until smooth. Puree cottage cheese in a blender or food processor, or press through a strainer until smooth. Beat pureed cottage cheese, cream cheese, chocolate mixture and almond extract with electric mixer until smooth. Fold into whipped cream. Spoon into a 1-quart coeur à la crème mold or colander lined with a double thickness of damp cheesecloth that hangs over sides. Fold cheesecloth over top. Let stand with weight on top. Drain in refrigerator at least 12 hours. Unmold and serve with fresh strawberries. Makes 6 servings.

Strawberry Cookie Tortes

Cookies all decked out in chocolate and strawberries.

Shortbread Cookies, see below
1 (10-oz.) pkg. frozen strawberries, thawed
1 tablespoon cornstarch
2 teaspoons grated orange peel
4 MILKY WAY Bars, cut up

2 tablespoons half-and-half
1/2 cup butter or margarine
1/3 cup whipping cream
Whipped cream for garnish

Shortbread Cookies:
2-1/4 cups flour
1/4 teaspoon salt
1 cup butter or margarine

1/2 cup powdered sugar
1 teaspoon vanilla extract

Prepare Shortbread Cookies. Drain strawberries; reserve syrup. In a small saucepan, combine reserved syrup and cornstarch. Stir until smooth. Cook, stirring constantly until thick and clear. Fold in strawberries and orange peel. Remove from heat. Chill. In a medium saucepan, combine candy and half-and-half. Melt over low heat, stirring until smooth. Cool to room temperature. In a large bowl, beat butter or margarine. Gradually add chocolate mixture, beating until light and creamy. To assemble each torte, spread one cookie with chocolate mixture and top with whipped cream. Spread a second cookie with strawberry mixture and carefully place on first cookie. Spread a third cookie with chocolate mixture and place on strawberry-topped cookie. Repeat to make 8 tortes. Chill. Let stand at room temperature 30 minutes before serving. Just before serving, top each torte with a dollop of whipped cream. Makes 8 servings.

Shortbread Cookies:
Preheat oven to 325°F (165°C). Stir together flour and salt. In a medium bowl, cream butter or margarine, sugar and vanilla until light and fluffy. Stir in flour mixture. Turn out on a lightly floured surface. Knead a few strokes and shape into a round patty. Wrap in plastic wrap or aluminum foil and chill about 1 hour. On a lightly floured surface, roll out half the dough to 1/4-inch thickness. Cut with fluted cookie cutters. Place on ungreased baking sheet. Bake 10 to 12 minutes or until light brown on edges. Cool. Makes about 24 cookies, depending on size of cutter.

For a tasty combination and contrast of textures, add crushed MUNCH Peanut Bars to fruit salad.

Valentine Cake

Dress up a cake mix for Valentine's Day or any day.

1 cup "M&M's" Plain Chocolate Candies
1/4 cup water
1/2 cup butter or margarine
2 teaspoons grated orange peel
5 cups powdered sugar

1/4 cup half-and-half
2 (9-in.) heart-shaped cake layers
"M&M's" Plain Chocolate Candies
   for decoration

In a small saucepan, combine 1 cup candies and water. Melt over low heat, stirring until smooth. Cool to room temperature, stirring several times, but do not allow to set. In a small bowl, beat butter or margarine until light. Gradually beat in orange peel, powdered sugar and half-and-half. Beat in chocolate mixture. Spread frosting between layers and frost top and sides of cake. Decorate with M&M's Plain Chocolate Candies, as desired. Makes one 9-inch cake.

Meringue Hearts With Chocolate Mousse

Meringue Hearts are fun, but you can make other shapes.

3 egg whites, room temperature
1 teaspoon vanilla extract
1/4 teaspoon cream of tartar
1/8 teaspoon salt

3/4 cup sugar
Chocolate Mousse, see below
Whipped Cream for garnish

Chocolate Mousse:
1 teaspoon unflavored gelatin
1/2 cup milk
3 3 MUSKETEERS Bars, cut up

1/2 teaspoon rum extract
Pinch salt
1 cup whipping cream, whipped

Preheat oven to 250°F (120°C). Cover 2 baking sheets with aluminum foil or heavy brown paper. Draw six 4-inch hearts on one sheet and six 6-inch arrows on the other. In a small bowl, combine egg whites and vanilla. Beat until frothy. Beat in cream of tartar and salt. Beat in sugar 1 table-spoonful at a time until sugar is dissolved and meringue is very stiff and glossy. Press about 1/3 cup meringue through small pastry tip to shape arrows. Pressing remaining meringue mixture through a large fluted tip, place a small amount in center of each heart. Spread out evenly to fill heart. Pipe remaining meringue around edge of heart. Bake 30 minutes. Turn off heat. Allow the arrows to dry out in oven 30 minutes longer and the meringue hearts 1-1/2 to 2 hours longer. Prepare Chocolate Mousse. Remove meringues from foil or paper. Spoon equal amounts of Chocolate Mousse into meringue hearts. Top with whipped cream. Break arrows in half and insert ends into chocolate mixture. Refrigerate until ready to serve. Makes 6 servings.

Chocolate Mousse:
In small saucepan, sprinkle gelatin in milk. Let stand 3 to 5 minutes. Add candy. Melt over low heat until candy and gelatin are dissolved and smooth. Stir in rum extract and salt. Cool until mixture begins to set. Fold whipped cream into candy mixture. Chill.

Peanut Meringue Bars

An easy treat for peanut lovers.

1-1/2 cups flour
1/2 teaspoon baking powder
1/2 teaspoon salt
1/2 cup butter or margarine
3/4 cup sugar

2 eggs, separated
1 teaspoon vanilla extract
1/8 teaspoon cream of tartar
1/4 cup light brown sugar, firmly packed
3 MUNCH Peanut Bars, finely chopped

Preheat oven to 325°F (165°C). Butter a 13" x 9" baking pan. Combine flour, baking powder and salt. In a large bowl, cream butter or margarine and sugar. Add egg yolks and vanilla. Beat until light and fluffy. Blend in flour mixture. Pat dough evenly over bottom of prepared pan. In a small bowl, beat egg whites and cream of tartar until soft peaks form when beater is lifted. Add brown sugar gradually and continue beating until stiff and glossy. Fold in chopped candy. Spread in an even layer over dough. Bake 25 minutes or until light brown. Cool. Makes 24 bars.

How To Make
Meringue Hearts With Chocolate Mousse

1/Draw heart shapes on brown paper or foil. Fill with a small amount of meringue, spreading evenly inside of out-line. With a pastry bag, pipe meringue around edges. Use about 1/3 cup meringue for each arrow.

2/Remove baked and cooled meringues. Fill the hearts with Chocolate Mousse. Place arrows on filling. Top with whip-ped cream.

Take A Cake And Make It Great

Be your own professional cake decorator! Start with a cake mix and end up with a unique treat. You'll be proud to say, "I did it myself!" Teenagers will enjoy the Chinese Checker Cake, page 39. Those who find the blend of orange and chocolate irresistible will rave about your Chocolate Orange Ribbon Cake, page 40. And what little girl could ever forget the Butterfly Cake, page 41, you made for her birthday!

Ladybug Cakes

Make one for each serving.

1 (about 18.5-oz.) pkg. yellow cake mix
Orange food coloring
1 (16-1/2-oz.) can ready-to-spread
   vanilla frosting

About 1 cup "M&M's" Plain Chocolate
   Candies
1 tube brown decorating gel
56 (6-in.) licorice sticks

Preheat oven to 350°F (175°C). Grease and flour eight 10-ounce glass baking dishes. Prepare cake according to package directions. Pour about 1/2 cup cake batter into each prepared baking dish. Bake 15 to 20 minutes or until light brown. Cool cakes 5 minutes. Remove from dishes. Cool completely on wire racks. With orange food coloring, tint frosting a pale orange. Spread top and sides of cakes with frosting. To make eyes, place 2 orange candies on one side of each cake. To outline shell wings, draw a line with decorating gel from the base of cake at the center to above an eye at the top. Continue line over top of cake to bottom of cake at back. Repeat process on other side. Place 3 rows of brown candies on each shell half. To make antennas, cut a 6-inch licorice stick in half. Place the halves right above eyes. Repeat for each cake. To make legs, bend 6 licorice pieces. Place 3 legs on each side of body. Repeat for each cake. Makes 8 cakes.

Fortress Cake

Children can help decorate this cake.

1 (about 18.5-oz.) pkg. yellow cake mix
1 (7.2-oz.) pkg. fluffy white frosting mix
1 MUNCH Peanut Bar
23 FUN SIZE Candies—MARATHON Bars
4 3 MUSKETEERS Bars

1 FUN SIZE Candy or 1/2 3 MUSKETTERS Bar
About 1/4 cup "M&M's" Plain Chocolate Candies
5 "M&M's" Peanut Chocolate Candies

Preheat oven to 350°F (175°C). Grease and flour a 13" x 9" baking pan. Prepare cake mix according to package directions. Bake in prepared pan as directed. Let stand in pan 10 minutes. Remove from pan and cool completely on wire rack. Cut a 2-inch strip off each narrow end of cake. Cut one strip in half crosswise. If cake has a rounded top, trim to make flat. Place the large square of cake on a tray. Prepare frosting mix according to package directions. Frost top and sides of cake. Arrange cake strips on top to form an X. Frost top and sides. Use MUNCH Peanut Bar as the drawbridge on one side of fortress. Stand the MARATHON Bars on end, pressing into frosting around edge. Stand a 3 MUSKETEERS Bar on end at each corner. Dab frosting on top of each 3 MUSKETEERS Bar and top with a peanut candy. Place a FUN SIZE or 1/2 of a 3 MUSKETEERS Bar in center of X. Top with peanut candy. To make windows, place plain candies along both sides of X base. Decorate top of X with a row of overlapping plain candies. Outline doorway at drawbridge with plain candies. Attach paper pennants with children's names or symbols to wooden picks into tops of large candy bars at corner of fortress and in bar in center of X. Makes 16 to 20 servings.

Milky Wonder Cake

That classic cake Grandma used to make.

6 MILKY WAY Bars
1 cup butter or margarine
2 cups sugar
4 eggs
1 teaspoon vanilla extract

2-1/2 cups flour
1/2 teaspoon baking soda
1-1/4 cups buttermilk
1 cup chopped nuts

Preheat oven to 350°F (175°C). Butter a 9-inch fluted tube pan. In a medium saucepan, combine candy and 1/2 cup of the butter or margarine. Melt over low heat, stirring until smooth. In a large mixer bowl, cream remaining 1/2 cup butter or margarine and sugar. Add eggs one at a time. Beat well after each addition. Add vanilla and melted candy. Beat until light and fluffy. Combine flour and baking soda. Add alternately with buttermilk to batter. Fold in nuts. Pour into prepared pan. Bake 1 hour and 20 minutes or until wooden pick inserted near center comes out dry. The top will be quite dark..Cool in pan 10 minutes. Remove from pan. Cool completely on wire rack. Frost, if desired. Makes 10 to 12 servings.

Balloon Cake

These balloons are good enough to eat!

2 (17-oz.) pkgs. pound cake mix
1 cup "M&M's" Plain Chocolate Candies,
   coarsely chopped
1 (7.2-oz.) pkg. fluffy white frosting mix

1 cup "M&M's" Plain Chocolate Candies
   for decorating
1/2 to 1 square unsweetened chocolate, melted
20 to 25 "M&M's" Peanut Chocolate Candies

Preheat oven to 350°F (175°C). Grease a 13" x 9" cake pan. In a large bowl, combine the 2 packages cake mix. Prepare according to package directions, adding ingredients called for on 2 packages of mix. Fold 1 cup coarsely chopped plain candies into batter. Pour into prepared pan. Bake 40 to 45 minutes or until wooden pick inserted in center comes out dry. Cool 5 minutes. Remove from pan and cool completely on wire rack. Prepare frosting according to package directions. Frost top and sides of cake. Press plain candies into frosting around top and bottom edges of cake. Make 3 strings with melted chocolate starting at one corner of cake. Arrange clusters of peanut candies on end of strings to resemble balloons. Makes 20 to 24 servings.

How To Make Balloon Cake

Press plain candies into frosting around edges and bottom of cake. Make 3 strings with melted chocolate. Arrange clusters of peanut candies to resemble ballons.

Pineapple Upside-Down Cake

A new addition to an old favorite.

1/4 cup butter or margarine
1 (20-oz.) can sliced pineapple,
   in natural juice
6 SNICKERS Bars, cut up

1 (about 18.5-oz.) pkg.
   yellow cake mix
Maraschino cherries

Preheat oven to 350°F (175°C). Melt butter or margarine in a 13" x 9" baking pan. Drain pineapple, reserving 1/2 cup of juice. In a small saucepan over low heat, melt bars with reserved pineapple juice, stirring until smooth. Prepare cake mix according to package directions. Spoon candy mixture into bottom of prepared baking pan. Arrange pineapple slices over candy mixture. Fill pineapple centers with cherries. Pour cake batter over all. Bake 30 to 35 minutes or until wooden pick inserted in center comes out dry. Immediately run knife around sides of cake and invert onto serving plate. Let stand 5 minutes before removing pan. Serve warm or at room temperature. Makes 16 to 20 servings.

Orange Blossom Cake

The distinctive flavor of orange and chocolate.

1 (about 18.5-oz.) pkg.
   yellow or white cake mix
1/3 cup sugar
1 tablespoon cornstarch
1/8 teaspoon salt
1/2 cup orange juice

1 egg, beaten
1 tablespoon grated orange peel
1 tablespoon butter or margarine
Orange-Chocolate Frosting, page 101
About 1/2 cup "M&M's" Plain
   Chocolate Candies

Prepare cake mix according to package directions. Pour into 2 greased and floured 9-inch, round cake pans. Bake according to package directions. Remove from pans. Cool on wire rack. In a medium saucepan, combine sugar, cornstarch and salt. Add orange juice and egg. Stir constantly over medium heat until thickened. Add orange peel and butter or margarine. Stir until butter or margarine is melted. Chill. Spread between cake layers. Frost top and sides of cake with Orange-Chocolate Frosting. Decorate top of cake with 2 rows of candies about 1 inch from edge of cake and around bottom of cake. Makes 10 to 12 servings.

Crunchy Peanut Cake

A peanut lover's dream.

2-1/2 cups flour
1 cup sugar
1 MUNCH Peanut Bar, crushed
1 tablespoon baking powder
1 teaspoon salt
1/2 cup shortening

1 cup milk
3 eggs
1 teaspoon vanilla extract
Crunchy Peanut Frosting, see below
1 MILKY WAY Bar, cut in pieces
1 tablespoon milk

Crunchy Peanut Frosting:
1 (about 15-oz.) pkg. vanilla frosting mix
2 MUNCH Peanut Bars, crushed

Preheat oven to 350°F (175°C). Grease and flour two 9-inch cake pans. In a large bowl, combine flour, sugar, crushed candy, baking powder, salt, shortening, milk, eggs and vanilla. With an electric mixer, beat at medium speed about 4 minutes. Pour into prepared pans. Bake 25 minutes or until wooden pick inserted in center comes out dry. Cool 10 minutes. Remove from pans. Cool on wire racks. Prepare Crunchy Peanut Frosting. Spread frosting on center, top and sides of cake. In a small saucepan, combine candy pieces with milk. Stir over low heat until smooth. Drizzle melted candy mixture over edge of cake. Makes one 9-inch cake.

Crunchy Peanut Frosting:
Prepare frosting according to package directions. Stir in crushed candy.

Coconut Topped Chocolate Cake

Make a hit with this at your next pot-luck.

1 (about 18.5-oz.) pkg. German chocolate
   cake mix
4 SNICKERS Bars, finely chopped

1/4 cup butter or margarine
1/2 cup flaked coconut

Grease and flour a 13" x 9" x 2" baking pan. Prepare cake mix according to package directions. Pour into prepared baking pan. Bake as directed. In a small saucepan, combine chopped candy and butter or margarine. Melt over low heat, stirring until smooth. Remove baked cake from oven and immediately spread chocolate mixture over top. Sprinkle with coconut. Cool. Makes 16 to 20 servings.

Variation

White, yellow or chocolate cake mix may be substituted for German chocolate cake mix.

Strawberry Chocolate Torte

Taste the yummy chocolate butter cream frosting.

1 (about 18.5-oz.) pkg. yellow cake mix
Chocolate Butter Cream Frosting, see below
1/2 cup strawberry preserves

4 3 MUSKETEERS Bars
12 whole strawberries, if desired

Chocolate Butter Cream Frosting:
3/4 cup "M&M's" Plain Chocolate Candies
3/4 cup milk
1/3 cup flour
2 teaspoons vanilla extract

1/4 teaspoon salt
1 cup butter, softened
1-1/4 cups powdered sugar

Preheat oven to 350°F (175°C). Grease and flour three 8-inch, round cake pans. Line prepared pans with wax paper. Prepare cake mix according to package directions. Pour into prepared pans. Bake 20 to 25 minutes or until wooden pick inserted near center comes out dry. Cool cake in pans 10 minutes. Remove from pans. Remove wax paper and cool cake completely on wire racks. Split each layer in half horizontally. Prepare Chocolate Butter Cream Frosting. To assemble cake, spread about 1/3 cup frosting between each layer. Frost sides but not top. Spread strawberry preserves on top. Cut candy bars through the top in half lengthwise. Turn cut side up and slice again in half lengthwise. There will be 4 narrow pieces with chocolate exterior intact. Place candy bar pieces around outside of cake, chocolate-side out, about 3/4 inch apart. Place whole berries on top around outer edge. Makes about 12 servings.

Chocolate Butter Cream Frosting:

In a medium saucepan, combine candies with 1/4 cup milk. Melt over low heat, stirring until smooth. Combine remaining milk with flour. Stir into chocolate mixture and continue to cook and stir until mixture thickens; add vanilla and salt. Cool slightly. In a small bowl, cream butter until light and fluffy. Gradually add powdered sugar. Beat well with electric mixer after each addition until light and fluffy. Add chocolate mixture. Beat at high speed until creamy. If mixture is thin, chill for a few minutes before spreading. Makes about 2-1/2 cups.

Variation

1/2 cup cherry preserves or cherry pudding and pie filling may be substituted for the strawberry preserves. Garnish with fresh cherries, if desired.

M&M/MARS products are designed to be stored at room temperature. If you refrigerate these candies, they may change in color, but the good taste remains the same.

Chinese Checker Cake

An easy design for party fun.

1 (about 18.5-oz.) pkg. yellow cake mix
1 (16-1/2-oz.) can ready-to-spread
   vanilla frosting
1 tube decorating gel

About 1 cup "M&M's" Plain Chocolate
   Candies
18 "M&M's" Peanut Chocolate Candies

Preheat oven to 350°F (175°C). Grease and flour a 14" x 2" pizza pan. Prepare cake mix according to package directions. Pour into prepared pan. Bake 25 to 30 minutes or until light brown. Let stand in pan 10 minutes. Remove from pan and cool completely on wire rack. Frost top and sides of cake with vanilla frosting. Smooth the frosting on top. Mark the outside edge with wooden picks at 6 equally spaced points. With a long knife or string, mark a straight line between every other pick to make a 6-pointed star. Follow these lines with decorating gel to mark a Chinese checkerboard. Arrange plain candies in points for a Chinese checker game. Use 10 plain candies of the same color for each section. Place assorted plain candies in 2 rows around sides of cake. Make flowers between points using 3 peanut candies for each flower. Makes 12-16 servings.

How To Make Chinese Checker Cake

With a wooden pick, mark outside edges of frosted cake at 6 equal points. Draw a straight line between every other point, making a 6-pointed star. Follow these lines with decorating gel. Arrange 10 plain candies in each section as shown. Decorate spaces between points and around cake's edge as desired.

Chocolate Pound Cake

Good with ice cream or fruit.

1 cup "M&M's" Plain Chocolate Candies	1/2 cup milk
3 tablespoons milk	2 eggs
1 (17-oz.) pkg. pound cake mix	Powdered sugar, if desired

Preheat oven to 350°F (175°C). Grease and flour a 9" x 5" loaf pan. In a small saucepan, combine candies and 3 tablespoons milk. Melt over low heat, stirring until smooth. Cool. In a large mixer bowl, combine cake mix and 1/2 cup milk. Add eggs. Beat 1 minute with electric mixer at medium speed. Stir in chocolate mixture. Pour into prepared loaf pan. Bake 60 to 70 minutes or until wooden pick inserted in center comes out dry. Sprinkle top with powdered sugar, if desired. Makes 10 servings.

Chocolate Orange Ribbon Cake

A marbled cake with a two-tone topping.

4 SNICKERS Bars, cut up	1 teaspoon grated orange peel
2 tablespoons milk	Fluffy Orange Frosting, see below
1 (about 18.5-oz.) pkg. yellow cake mix	Chocolate Glaze, see below

Fluffy Orange Frosting:

1 (7.2-oz.) pkg. fluffy white frosting mix	1 teaspoon grated orange peel
1/2 cup orange juice	

Chocolate Glaze:
2 SNICKERS Bars, cut up
1 tablespoon milk

Preheat oven to 350°F (175°C). Grease and flour two 9-inch cake pans. In a small saucepan, combine candy and milk. Melt over low heat, stirring until smooth. Cool to room temperature. Prepare cake mix according to package directions. Divide batter in half. Stir candy mixture into half the batter. Stir grated orange peel into remaining half. Spoon chocolate and yellow batters alternately into cake pans. Bake 30 to 35 minutes or until wooden pick inserted in center comes out dry. Let stand in pans 10 minutes. Remove cakes and cool completely on wire racks. Make Fluffy Orange Frosting. Spread between layers and on top and sides of cake. Make Chocolate Glaze. Drizzle in a circle around edge of cake, allowing it to run down sides. Makes 10 to 12 servings.

Fluffy Orange Frosting:
Prepare frosting mix according to package directions, substituting orange juice for water called for on package. Stir in orange peel.

Chocolate Glaze:
In a small saucepan, combine candy and milk. Melt over low heat, stirring until smooth. Cool just until it can be easily drizzled on top of cake.

Butterfly Cake

Perfect for a little girl's birthday party.

1 (9-in.) round baked yellow cake layer
1 (7.2-oz.) pkg. fluffy white frosting mix
2 MARATHON Bars
About 3/4 cup brown "M&M's"
    Plain Chocolate Candies

2 orange "M&M's" Peanut Chocolate Candies
24 STARBURST Fruit Chews, cut in half

Cut cake layer in half crosswise. Prepare frosting mix according to package directions. Arrange cake pieces on tray with rounded edges facing each other, about 1/2 inch apart. Frost cake. To make butterfly body and antennas, stand both candy bars on edge between cake layers with about 1/2 of each candy bar extended above the cake. Press cake pieces against the candy bars. Curve the ends of candy bars apart slightly. To decorate wings, outline around edge of cake pieces and through center with plain candies, alternating light and dark brown. Alternate light and dark brown plain candies around base of cake. Place the 2 peanut candies between wings at base of antennas for eyes. Arrange STARBURST Fruit Chews on wings. Makes 8 to 12 servings.

How To Make Butterfly Cake

Place rounded edges of cake together and frost. Place candy bars on end between the cake edges to form butterfly body. Arrange fruit chews on wings and decorate with plain candies as shown in photograph.

41

Cottage Cake

Delightful to look at, delicious to taste.

3 (18.5-oz.) pkgs. white cake mix
1-1/3 cups white vegetable shortening
2 lbs. powdered sugar, sifted
2 teaspoons vanilla
4 to 6 tablespoons milk

13-in. square heavy cardboard
Large sheet heavy duty aluminum foil
1 can spreadable chocolate frosting
2 (1 lb.) pkgs. "M&M's" Plain Chocolate
   Candies

Prepare cake mixes according to package directions. Bake each cake in a 11" x 7" baking pan according to baking instructions on package. Cool baked cakes on wire racks. Cut each cake in half, forming six 7" x 5-1/2" cake layers. With an electric mixer, cream the shortening in a large mixing bowl. Add powdered sugar 1/2 cup at a time. Continue beating until all sugar is used. Beat in vanilla and enough milk to make frosting a spreadable consistency. Cover cardboard square with aluminum foil. On foil-covered board, assemble bottom of house by stacking 3 cake layers with white frosting between layers. The 7-inch sides are the front and back of house. To shape roof, stack 2 layers and trim at an angle to form the peak. If necessary, level house by trimming top layer or reversing the roof layers. Spread frosting between roof layers. Place both layers on top of house, spreading frosting between house and roof. Fill in any spaces with frosting to even sides and seams of house. Frost the front, back and sides with white frosting. Frost roof with chocolate frosting. With a toothpick mark door and window designs on house. Fit pastry bag with fine plain tip and fill with chocolate frosting. Outline doors and windows similar to those pictured with chocolate frosting. If frosting has set, apply dab of white frosting to back of "M&M's" Candies before pressing in place. If desired, use a fine star tip and chocolate frosting to add a row of stars to each corner of house. Use a large star tip and white frosting to add row of stars around bottom of house. While frosting is still soft, insert green, yellow and orange "M&M's" Candies. Using large star tip and chocolate frosting, outline roof with star tip border. If desired, decorate peak and roof with scallops of white frosting. Further decorating of the house and yard can be done as shown in the photo or finished as desired.

Festive Frosted Loaf Cake

Colorful candies add crunch and flavor.

1 (10-3/4 oz.) pound cake
1 (7.2 oz.) pkg. fluffy white
   frosting mix

1 cup "M&M's" Peanut Chocolate Candies,
   chopped
1/2 teaspoon orange extract

Cut cake horizontally into 3 even layers. Prepare frosting mix according to package directions. Reserve 1 to 2 tablespoons chopped candies for decorating top of cake. Fold remaining chopped candies and orange extract into frosting mix. Spread frosting between cake layers. Frost top and sides of cake. Sprinkle top with reserved chopped candies. Makes 6 to 8 servings.

Variation
"M&M's" Plain Chocolate Candies may be substituted for "M&M's" Peanut Chocolate Candies.

1/Generously spread frosting between 3 of the cake layers and stack them to form the base for the house.

2/For roof, spread frosting between 2 more cake layers. Cut with a bread knife from the top at a sharp angle, through both layers. Leave a small flat peak.

How To Make Cottage Cake

3/Place the 2 roof layers on top of house base. If necessary to level the house, reverse the roof layers from front to back. Spread white frosting over front, back and sides of house.

4/Cover roof with chocolate frosting. Use a wooden pick to draw doors and windows as desired. Decorate over lines with chocolate frosting. Spread white frosting on foil around the house. Create your own yard with candies and cookies.

Triple-Decker Cake

A 3-layer beauty!

7 3 MUSKETEERS Bars
1/4 cup water
3/4 cup butter or margarine
1 cup sugar
1 teaspoon vanilla extract
3 eggs

2-1/2 cups flour
1 teaspoon baking soda
1 teaspoon salt
2/3 cup water
Butter Cream Frosting, see below

Butter Cream Frosting:
1/3 cup butter or margarine, softened
1 (1-lb.) box powdered sugar
1 teaspoon vanilla extract

1/4 teaspoon salt
1/4 to 1/2 cup milk

Preheat oven to 350°F (175°C). Grease and flour three 8-inch, round cake pans. Line with wax paper. Freeze 1 whole candy bar. Cut remaining bars into chunks. In a medium saucepan, combine chunked candy and 1/4 cup water. Melt over low heat, stirring until smooth. Cool. In a medium bowl, cream butter or margarine, sugar and vanilla. Add eggs one at a time, beating well after each addition. Beat until mixture is light and fluffy. Stir in chocolate mixture. Stir together flour, baking soda and salt. Add to chocolate mixture alternately with 2/3 cup water, beginning and ending with flour mixture. Pour into prepared pans. Bake 30 to 35 minutes or until wooden pick inserted near center comes out dry. Remove from oven. Cool 5 minutes. Remove cake from pans. Cool on wire racks. Prepare Butter Cream Frosting. Frost the top of each layer with approximately 1/3 of the frosting. Assemble cake. Chop frozen candy bar in blender, food processor or by hand. Sprinkle over top layer. Makes one 8-inch cake or 10 to 12 servings.

Butter Cream Frosting:
In a large mixer bowl, beat butter or margarine and 1 cup powdered sugar until light. Add vanilla, salt and 3 tablespoons milk. Beat well. Add remaining sugar and milk as needed for spreading consistency.

Everybody remembers "S'Mores" from Scouting days. Try a chocolate-nougat "S'More" made by sandwiching a hot marshmallow and a slice of SNICKERS or MILKY WAY Bar between two graham crackers.

Easter

These recipes will make your festivities memorable, from the children's Easter baskets and something special for Easter breakfast to a fabulous holiday dessert. Start with edible Easter Cookie Baskets, below, or fill big straw baskets with Easter Cookie Fantasies, page 55. Easter Bunny Cake, page 52, or a Bavarian Easter Egg, page 54, will provide the perfect ending to your gala dinner. Or serve the Chocolate Cheese Egg, page 48, and coffee for a light dessert.

Easter Cookie Baskets

An edible Easter basket filled with candies.

1 (3-1/2-oz.) can flaked coconut
Green food coloring
1-1/2 cups flour
1/4 teaspoon salt
3/4 cup butter or margarine
1/2 cup sugar

1 egg, separated
1 teaspoon vanilla extract
1/4 cup "M&M's" Peanut Chocolate Candies, chopped
Additional "M&M's" Peanut Chocolate Candies

To tint coconut, mix a small amount of water and green food coloring in a large bowl. Add coconut and toss with a fork until coconut is evenly colored. Spread on paper toweling until dry. Preheat oven to 350°F (175°C). Stir together flour and salt. In a large bowl, cream butter or margarine and sugar. Add egg yolk and vanilla. Beat until creamy. Add flour mixture gradually. Stir in chopped candies. Chill dough until it can be handled easily, about 30 minutes. Shape dough into balls, using a tablespoonful of dough for each ball. Dip in egg white. Roll in coconut, pressing coconut onto ball. Place on ungreased baking sheet. Using thumb or the back of a 1/2 teaspoon measuring spoon, make a deep indentation in center of each ball. Bake about 15 minutes or until light brown. Remove from baking sheets. Cool on wire rack. Fill centers with whole candies. Makes 30 cookies.

Easter Basket Cake

Your family will love this Easter treat.

1 (about 18.5-oz.) pkg. yellow or white
   cake mix
1 (7.2-oz.) pkg. fluffy white frosting mix
About 1-1/2 cups "M&M's" Plain Chocolate
   Candies

About 1/2 cup "M&M's" Peanut Chocolate
   Candies (30 candies)
Green decorating gel

Preheat oven to 350°F (175°C). Grease and flour a 13" x 9" baking pan. Prepare cake mix according to package directions. Bake as directed. Cool cake in pan 10 minutes. Remove from pan and cool completely on wire rack. Prepare frosting mix according to package directions. Frost sides and top of cake. Outline basket and handle on top of cake with tip of knife. To make basket, outline the top row with dark brown plain candies, standing candies on edge. Make second row with light brown plain candies lying flat. Alternate rows of dark and light brown plain candies to complete basket. Outline sides of basket with dark brown plain candies standing on edge. To make basket handle, alternate brown and yellow plain candies. Use green plain candies for grass in basket. Make clusters of flowers in basket with orange and yellow peanut candies and stems with green decorating gel. Make a cluster of flowers in each corner of cake, if desired. Arrange assorted plain candies around sides of cake, overlapping candies slightly. Makes 16 to 20 servings.

How To Make Easter Basket Cake

Use a wooden pick to outline a basket and handle on the frosted cake. Arrange brown candies to form basket and handle. Use green decorating gel for flower stems and grass. Create clusters of flowers in basket and on corners, edges and sides.

Bunny & Duck Easter Breads

Perfect Easter breakfast rolls.

1 (13-3/4-oz.) pkg. hot roll mix	1/3 cup chopped candied cherries
3/4 cup warm water (110°F, 45°C)	1/3 cup "M&M's" Plain Chocolate Candies
1 teaspoon vanilla extract	chopped
1/4 cup butter or margarine, softened	Powdered Sugar Icing, page 102
2 tablespoons sugar	Additional "M&M's" Plain or Peanut
1 egg	Chocolate Candies

In a large bowl, combine yeast from hot roll mix with 3/4 cup warm water. Let stand 3 to 5 minutes. Add vanilla extract. Beat in butter or margarine, sugar, egg and candied cherries. Stir in flour mixture from hot roll mix. Cover dough and let rise in warm place until double in bulk, about 45 minutes. Knead dough on lightly floured surface until smooth, about 10 to 12 strokes. Roll into a circle about 12 inches in diameter. Sprinkle with chopped candies; press into dough. Fold dough in thirds and press down. Grease a baking sheet. Divide dough into 8 portions. Roll each portion into a rope 18 inches long. Cut several 1-inch lengths from the end of dough pieces, depending on design to be made. On prepared baking sheet, shape each long piece of dough into a figure 8 design, using 1/3 of the dough for the head and the remaining dough for the body. For the Bunny: Shape three 1-inch pieces of dough for the ears and tail. Press to attach to figure 8's. For the Duck: Shape 2 end pieces of dough for the beak and twist for the feet. Press to attach to figure 8's. Shape dough for tail. Make a deep indentation in the heads and bodies of dough figures and fill with a ball of foil, pressing it down well. Let rise until doubled in bulk, 20 to 30 minutes. Meanwhile, preheat oven to 350°F (175°C). Bake 15 to 18 minutes until golden brown. Remove balls of foil. Cool bread figures on wire rack. Frost with Powdered Sugar Icing and fill indentations with "M&M's" Plain or Peanut Chocolate Candies. Makes 8 bunnies or 8 ducks.

Variations

Quick Easter Stollen: Substitute 2 teaspoons orange peel for chopped candied cherries. Increase candies to 1/2 cup. Sprinkle dough with 1/2 of the chopped candies; press into dough and fold in thirds. Roll out and repeat using remaining candies. Roll dough into 12" x 9" oval. Fold in half lengthwise, bringing top to within 1/2 inch of opposite side. Place on greased baking sheet. Let rise until doubled in bulk, about 30 minutes. Preheat oven to 350°F (175°C). Bake 35 to 40 minutes or until light brown. Cool on wire rack. Frost with Powdered Sugar Icing and sprinkle with chopped candies. Makes 1 coffeecake about 12 inches long.

Easter Ring: Divide dough in half. Roll each half into a rope about 24 inches long. Place ropes together and twist, then bring ends together to make an 8-inch circle. Place on greased baking sheet. Make 6 deep indentations in dough and fill each with large ball of foil, pressing down firmly. Let rise until doubled in size, about 30 minutes. Meanwhile, preheat oven to 350°F (175°C). Press foil balls down again. Bake 25 to 30 minutes or until light brown. Remove balls of foil. Cool on wire rack. Frost with Powdered Sugar Icing. Fill indentations with "M&M's" Peanut Chocolate Candies. Makes 1 coffeecake.

Chocolate Cheese Egg

Entertain with fruit and cheese in a festive shape.

1 (12-oz.) pkg. "M&M's" Plain Chocolate
   Candies
3 tablespoons milk

2 (8-oz.) pkgs. cream cheese, softened
Fresh fruit and crackers

Reserve 1/2 cup each orange, green and yellow candies. In a small saucepan combine the remaining candies with milk. Melt over low heat, stirring until smooth. In a medium mixing bowl, beat cheese until smooth. Beat in melted chocolate. Chill in freezer 2 or 3 hours. Form into egg shape. Press reserved candies into surface of chocolate egg in a decorative design. Refrigerate until serving time. Serve with fresh fruit and crackers. Makes 1 chocolate-cheese egg, about 6 inches long.

Choco-Banana Muffins

Delicious with a tall glass of cold milk.

1 (15-oz.) pkg. banana bread mix
2 MILKY WAY Bars, cut in small pieces

Preheat oven to 375°F (190°C). Line 12 muffin cups with paper or foil liners. Prepare bread mix according to package directions for muffins. Stir in chopped candy bars. Fill each prepared muffin cup 2/3 full. Bake 20 to 25 minutes. Makes 12 muffins.

Tangy Topped Cheesecake

Add distinctive flavor to a cheesecake mix.

1 (14.8-oz) pkg. no-bake cheesecake mix
1 (8-oz.) pkg. STARBURST Fruit Chews

2 tablespoons water

Prepare crust from mix according to package directions. Reserve 2 tablespoons crumb mixture. Press remaining mixture into a 9-inch pie pan. In a medium saucepan, combine candies and water. Melt over low heat, stirring until smooth. Prepare cheesecake filling according to package directions. Stir in melted candy. Pour into crust. Prepare topping; spread over filling. Sprinkle with reserved crumbs. Chill at least 2 hours. Refrigerate until ready to serve. Makes 6 to 8 servings.

Cookie-Topped Cupcakes

Candied cupcakes make adorable centerpieces.

1 (17-oz.) pkg. pound cake mix
1/2 cup chopped "M&M's" Plain Chocolate
  Candies
1 (7.2-oz.) pkg. fluffy white frosting mix or
  1 recipe favorite 7-minute frosting recipe

Additional "M&M's" Plain Chocolate Candies
Tiny frosted chicken or duck cookies made
  from Easter Cookie Fantasies, page 55

Preheat oven to 350°F (175°C). Grease twelve 2- to 2-1/2-inch muffin cups or 15 to 18 smaller ones. Prepare pound cake batter according to package directions. Fold chopped candies into batter. Pour into prepared muffin cups. Bake 20 to 25 minutes for large cupcakes, 18 to 20 minutes for small ones. Cool in pan 5 minutes. Remove from pan and cool on wire rack. Prepare frosting according to package directions. Frost top of each cupcake generously. Decorate edge of tops with candies. Just before serving, stand a frosted chicken or duck cookie upright in center. Makes 12 large cupcakes or 15 to 18 small cupcakes.

Easter Fruit Bread

An updated version of a traditional Russian Easter bread.

1 (13-3/4-oz.) pkg. hot roll mix
1/2 cup warm water (110°F, 45°C)
1/4 cup butter or margarine
2 tablespoons sugar
2 eggs
1 teaspoon vanilla extract
1/2 teaspoon rum extract

1/4 cup golden raisins
1/4 cup mixed candied fruit
1/2 cup "M&M's" Peanut Chocolate Candies,
  chopped
3/4 cup Powdered Sugar Icing, page 102
Additional "M&M's" Peanut Chocolate
  Candies, if desired

In a large mixing bowl, combine yeast from hot roll mix and warm water. Let stand 3 to 5 minutes. Beat in butter or margarine, sugar, eggs, vanilla and rum extracts. Stir in flour mixture from hot roll mix. Add raisins and candied fruit. Cover and let rise in warm place until doubled in size, 45 to 60 minutes. Knead dough on lightly floured surface until smooth and elastic. Roll into a circle about 12 inches in diameter. Sprinkle chopped candies evenly over top; press into dough. Fold dough into thirds and press together. Cut off 1/3 of dough. Shape each portion of dough into a round. Place larger portion in greased 1-lb. coffee can and smaller portion in greased 16-oz. vegetable or fruit can (about 2 cups). Let dough rise in warm place until doubled. Preheat oven to 350°F (175°C). Bake 30 to 35 minutes for smaller loaf, 40 to 45 minutes for larger loaf, or until done. If top browns before bread is fully baked, cover with foil tent. Remove from cans and cool 10 to 15 minutes on wire racks. Frost tops of loaves with Powdered Sugar Icing, allowing some icing to drizzle down sides of loaf. Sprinkle with additional chopped candies, if desired. Makes 1 large and 1 small loaf.

Chocolate Nests

Crunchy noodles and chocolate will surprise you.

1 cup "M&M's" Plain Chocolate Candies
2 tablespoons water
1 (3-oz.) can chow mein noddles, slightly
   broken

2/3 cup Green Coconut, see below
"M&M's" Peanut Chocolate Candies, as desired

Green Coconut:
2 tablespoons water
2 to 3 drops green food coloring

2/3 cup flaked coconut

On wax paper or foil-lined baking sheets, draw 6 circles 2-1/2 to 3 inches in diameter. In a small saucepan, combine candies and water. Stir over low heat until smooth. Carefully stir in noodles. Following outlines on wax paper, shape into nests. Work quickly because chocolate hardens rapidly. Let stand at room temperature. Fill nests with green flaked coconut and peanut candies. Makes 6 nests.

Green Coconut:
In a small bowl, combine water and green food coloring. Add flaked coconut. Toss with a fork until coconut is evenly colored. Spread on a tray lined with double thickness of paper toweling. Let dry. Unused Green Coconut can be stored in an airtight container in freezer.

How To Make Chocolate Nests

1/Draw six 3-inch circles on waxed paper or foil. Spoon mixture onto each circle. Working quickly with a spoon, form a nest, following outlines. Let stand at room temperature until firm.

2/Fill nests with green tinted coconut and peanut candies.

Easter Bunny Cake

Chocolate Candies make quick decorations for this Easter cake.

1 (about 18.5-oz.) pkg. yellow cake mix
1 (7.2-oz.) pkg. fluffy white frosting mix
3 "M&M's" Peanut Chocolate Candies

About 1-1/2 cups "M&M's" Plain Chocolate
    Candies

Preheat oven to 350°F (175°C). Grease and flour one 9-inch and one 8-inch, round cake pan. Prepare cake mix according to package directions. Pour into prepared cake pans. Bake 25 to 35 minutes or until wooden pick inserted in center comes out dry. Cool in pans 10 minutes. Remove from pans and cool on wire racks. Prepare frosting mix according to package directions. Cut the 8-inch cake in half crosswise, then cut a strip 2 inches wide from cut edge of each half to use for ears. Place the 9-inch cake on a large tray, at least 17" x 12". Arrange the 2 strips on one side of the round cake for the ears. Opposite the ears, arrange the remaining pieces of cake, rounded side down, to make a bow tie. Frost sides and top of all cake pieces. Use 2 brown peanut candies for eyes, an orange peanut candy for the nose and 5 orange plain candies for the mouth. For whiskers, stand dark brown plain candies on edge in rows starting from the nose. Fill in centers of ears with 2 rows of orange plain candies. Outline the bow tie with rows of assorted plain candies around top and sides. Outline the bunny head around sides of cake with assorted plain candies. Makes one 17" x 12" cake.

Fluted Orange Bread

Hot roll mix is the base of this easy holiday bread.

2 (13-3/4-oz.) pkgs. hot roll mix
1 cup warm water, (110°F, 45°C)
1/2 cup butter or margarine
1/4 cup sugar
2 eggs
1 tablespoon grated orange peel

3/4 cup "M&M's" Peanut Chocolate Candies,
    chopped
Powdered Sugar Icing, page 102
Additional "M&M's" Plain or Peanut
    Chocolate Candies, chopped

Grease a 10-inch Bundt pan. In a large mixing bowl, combine yeast from 2 packages hot roll mix in warm water. Let stand about 5 minutes. Beat in butter or margarine, sugar, eggs and orange peel. Add flour mixture from hot roll mixes; mix well. Cover dough and let rise in warm place until doubled in bulk, about 45 minutes. On a lightly floured surface, knead until smooth and elastic. Spoon about 1/4 of the dough into prepared pan. Sprinkle with about 1/3 chopped candies. Repeat 2 times. Spoon remaining dough on top. Let dough rise until doubled in size. Preheat oven to 350°F (175°C). Bake 45 minutes or until light brown. Let stand in pan about 5 minutes. Remove from pan and cool on wire rack. Frost with Powdered Sugar Icing and sprinkle with chopped candies. Makes 10 to 12 servings.

Variation

Omit orange peel. Substitute 1 teaspoon vanilla extract and 1/2 teaspoon rum extract. Fold 1/4 cup raisins and 1/4 cup mixed candied fruits into hot roll mix.

Sitting Pretties

Great treats anytime.

1/2 cup butter or margarine
1/4 cup brown sugar, firmly packed
1 egg, separated
1/2 teaspoon vanilla extract
1 cup flour

1/4 teaspoon salt
About 1/4 cup finely chopped nuts
1 (16.5-oz.) can vanilla creamy-type frosting
About 24 "M&M's" Plain or Peanut Chocolate
     Candies

In a large bowl, cream butter or margarine and sugar. Beat in egg yolk and vanilla. Stir in flour and salt. Chill 1 hour. Preheat oven to 350°F (175°C). Grease baking sheets. Roll dough into 1-inch balls. In a small bowl, slightly beat egg white. Dip each ball into egg white then roll in chopped nuts. Place 1 inch apart on prepared baking sheet. Bake 5 minutes. Press thumb gently in center of each and bake 5 minutes longer. Cool. Fill thumbprint with frosting. Garnish with candies. Makes about 24 cookies.

How To Make Sitting Pretties

1/Roll dough into 1-inch balls. Dip first into slightly beaten egg white and then roll in nuts. Place 1 inch apart on prepared baking sheet.

2/Bake 5 minutes. Press thumb gently in center of each cookie. Continue baking. When cool, fill centers with frosting and top with peanut candies.

Bavarian Easter Egg

A different, delicious do-ahead dessert.

4 eggs, separated
1 cup milk
1/4 teaspoon salt
1 tablespoon (1 envelope) unflavored gelatin
1-1/4 cups "M&M's" Plain Chocolate Candies
2 tablespoons sugar

1 teaspoon vanilla extract
1/2 teaspoon rum extract
1 cup (1/2 pint) whipping cream, whipped
3/4 to 1 cup whipping cream, whipped
About 1 cup "M&M's" Plain Chocolate Candies

In a small bowl, beat egg yolks slightly. In a medium saucepan, combine beaten yolks, milk, salt and gelatin. Add candies. Melt over low heat. Stir until mixture is smooth and thickened. Do not boil. Chill until mixture begins to set. In a deep bowl, beat egg whites until they form soft peaks when beater is lifted. Add sugar gradually and continue beating until glossy. Beat chilled gelatin mixture until smooth. Beat in vanilla and rum extract. Fold in egg whites, then 2 cups whipped cream. Pour into a 6-cup melon mold. Chill until firm. Unmold onto serving plate. To decorate, draw light diagonal lines 1-1/2 inches apart on mold. With remaining whipped cream, pipe rosettes through pastry tube along lines and around bottom edge. Press candies into each rosette and around bottom. Refrigerate until serving time. Makes 6 to 8 servings.

Variation

Any shape 6-cup mold can be used. Decorate as desired with whipped cream and candies.

Dogwood Blossoms

Festive flowers made from refrigerated cookie dough.

1 (18-oz.) roll refrigerated sugar cookie dough

About 3/4 cup "M&M's" Plain Chocolate Candies

Preheat oven to 350°F (175° C). Slice cookie dough 1/4-inch thick. To form 4 flower petals, cut 4 tiny wedges of dough about 1/2 inch deep from around edge of each slice. Place slices on ungreased baking sheet, 6 at a time. Bake about 10 minutes or until light brown. Press orange or yellow candies in each of the 4 flower petals and 1 light brown candy in center as soon as they are taken out of oven. Remove cookies carefully and cool on wire rack. Makes about 36 cookies.

Variation

Quick Version: Cut 4 wedges along the whole cookie dough roll. Then cut into 1/4-inch thick slices.

Easy Pear Kuchen

Try this fruit dessert a la mode.

4 3 MUSKETEERS Bars	1/2 cup rolled oats
1/4 cup milk	1/4 cup brown sugar, firmly packed
1 teaspoon ground cinnamon	1/4 cup butter or margarine
1 (29-oz.) can pear halves, drained	Vanilla ice cream, if desired
1/2 cup flour	

Preheat oven to 375°F (190°C). In a small saucepan, combine candy, milk and cinnamon. Melt over low heat, stirring until smooth. Arrange pear halves in bottom of an 8-inch square baking pan. Pour chocolate mixture over pears. In a medium bowl, combine flour, oats, brown sugar and butter or margarine. Sprinkle mixture over pears and chocolate. Bake 30 to 35 minutes. Serve warm with vanilla ice cream, if desired. Makes 8 servings.

Easter Cookie Fantasies

Use this for any cut-out shape.

2-1/2 cups flour	2 tablespoons milk
1-1/2 cups sifted powdered sugar	2 teaspoons vanilla extract
1/2 teaspoon salt	Powdered Sugar Icing, page 102, or Orange
1 cup butter or margarine	Chocolate Frosting, page 101
1 egg, beaten	"M&M's" Plain Chocolate Candies, as desired

In a large mixing bowl, stir together flour, powdered sugar and salt. Cut in butter or margarine until mixture resembles coarse crumbs. Add beaten egg, milk and vanilla. Mix until dough holds together. Press into a ball. Wrap in foil or plastic wrap and chill. Preheat oven to 325°F (165°C). On lightly floured surface, roll out 1/2 dough at a time 1/8 to 1/4 inch thick. Cut into desired shapes with cookie cutter. Place on ungreased cookie sheets. Bake 8 to 10 minutes. Cool on wire racks. Frost as desired. Decorate with candies. Makes 24 to 48 cookes.

Variation

Big Bunny Cookies: Add 1 teaspoon orange extract to cookie dough recipe. Make Big Bunny Cookie pattern by drawing a 3-1/2-inch circle on cardboard using an inverted plate or bowl. Draw 2 ears about 3 inches tall and 3/4 inch wide. Cut out cardboard shape. Place pattern on dough and cut around edge with a sharp pointed knife. Carefully transfer cookies with 1 or 2 large spatulas to ungreased baking sheets. Bake according to recipe above. Decorate with candies to make eyes, nose and mouth. Makes 8 to 10 cookies.

Hot Cross Buns

A favorite Easter roll made better with chocolate.

1 (13-3/4-oz.) pkg. hot roll mix
3/4 cup warm water (110°F, 45°C)
1/4 cup butter or margarine
2 tablespoons sugar
1 egg
1 teaspoon grated lemon peel
1/2 teaspoon ground cinnamon

1/4 teaspoon ground nutmeg
1/3 cup currants
1/2 cup "M&M's" Plain Chocolate Candies, chopped
1 tablespoon sugar
1 tablespoon milk
Powdered Sugar Icing, page 102

In a large mixing bowl, combine yeast from hot roll mix and warm water. Let stand about 5 minutes. Beat in butter or margarine, 2 tablespoons sugar, egg, lemon peel, cinnamon and nutmeg. Gradually beat in flour mixture from hot roll mix. Stir in currants. Knead dough on lightly floured surface until smooth and elastic. Cover and let rise in warm place until doubled in bulk about 45 minutes. Grease 2 baking sheets. Roll dough into circle about 12 inches in diameter. Sprinkle chopped candies evenly over top; press into dough; Fold dough in thirds and press down. Divide dough into 18 equal portions. Shape each portion into a ball. Place on greased baking sheets. Let rise until doubled in size. Preheat oven to 350°F (175°C). Bake 20 to 25 minutes. Stir together 1 tablespoon sugar and the milk. Brush over hot buns. Remove buns from pans and cool on wire rack. Make a cross with Powdered Sugar Icing on top of each bun. Makes 18 buns.

Coconut Cream Pie

Toasted coconut with a crunchy peanut crust.

4 MUNCH Peanut Bars, crushed
1 cup graham cracker crumbs (about 12 crackers)
1/4 cup butter or margarine, melted

1 (3-5/8-oz.) pkg. coconut pudding and pie filling
1/2 cup shredded coconut

Preheat oven to 400°F (205°C). In a medium bowl, combine crushed candy, graham cracker crumbs and butter or margarine. Press into a 9-inch pie pan. Bake 5 minutes. Cool. Prepare pie filling according to package directions. Cool 5 minutes. Toast coconut under broiler until light brown. Spoon filling into pie shell. Sprinkle toasted coconut over top. Chill. Refrigerate until ready to serve. Makes 6 to 8 servings.

Crush MUNCH Peanut Bars by placing chunks of candy bars in food processor or blender, or crush with rolling pin until coarse crumbs form.

Easter Flower Pot Breads

A novel idea for a holiday bake sale.

2 (4-inch) clay flower pots, seasoned, see below
1 (13-3/4-oz.) pkg. hot roll mix
2/3 cup warm water (110°F, 45°C)
2 tablespoons sugar
2 tablespoons butter or margarine, softened
1 egg
1/2 teaspoon grated lemon peel

1/2 teaspoon ground cardamom
1/2 cup chopped mixed candied fruit
1/2 cup "M&M's" Plain Chocolate Candies,
  chopped
Powdered Sugar Frosting, see below
Additional "M&M's" Plain Chocolate Candies

Powdered Sugar Frosting:
1/2 cup powdered sugar
1-1/2 teaspoons butter or margarine

1-1/2 teaspoons milk
Additional "M&M's" Plain Chocolate Candies

Season clay pots. In a large mixing bowl, combine yeast from hot roll mix with warm water. Let stand 3 to 4 minutes. Beat in sugar, butter or margarine, egg, lemon peel and cardamom. Stir in flour mixture from hot roll mix. Add candied fruits. Cover and let rise in warm place until doubled in bulk, about 45 minutes. Knead dough on a lightly floured surface until smooth and elastic. Roll into a 12-inch circle. Sprinkle evenly with chopped candies and press them into dough. Fold dough into thirds and press down. Divide into 2 equal portions. Shape each portion into round loaf. Line seasoned pots with greased wax paper. Place each round in prepared pot. Let rise until double in bulk, about 1 inch above top of pot. Bake in preheated 350°F (175°C) oven 25 minutes. Cover top with foil tent and continue baking 15 minutes more. Let stand 5 to 10 minutes. Loosen bread carefully around sides before removing from pots. Peel off paper. Cool on wire racks. Breads may be prepared up to this point and wrapped in foil and frozen. Return to pots and frost with Powdered Sugar Frosting. Decorate with additional whole candies. Makes 2 loaves.

Clay Pot Seasoning:

To season clay pots for baking, thoroughly wash in warm water. Grease interior surface with shortening. Place on baking sheet. Preheat oven to 350°F (175°C) and bake pots 10 minutes. Remove from oven and cool slightly. Repeat greasing with shortening on interior and baking 3 more times. Cool before using.

Powdered Sugar Frosting:

In a medium mixing bowl beat sugar, butter or margarine and milk until smooth. Frost tops and decorate with additional whole candies.

The chocolate coating protects the fresh flavor and soft texture in nougat-centered bars. Once the chocolate coating is broken, the nougat will dry out, so enjoy promptly.

Elegant Desserts

These delectable, sophisticated desserts add glamour to a dress-up family affair, impress guests at a formal dinner or give a romantic flair to a small supper. Chilled Mocha Soufflé, page 60, will be everyone's favorite. The famous Pears Hélène, page 62, takes only moments to make. And for a truly superb dessert, try Marmalade Crepes, page 63.

Peanutty Angel-Food Cake

Texture plus taste equals delicious.

1 tablespoon (1 envelope) unflavored gelatin
1/4 cup cold water
2 tablespoons orange juice
1 teaspoon vanilla extract
8 egg yolks

1 cup powdered sugar
2 cups whipping cream, whipped
1 (10-in.) angel-food cake
4 MUNCH Peanut Bars, coarsely ground

In a small saucepan, combine gelatin and water. Let stand about 3 minutes. Place over low heat, stirring until gelatin is dissolved. Add orange juice and vanilla. Cool slightly. In a large mixing bowl, beat egg yolks until thick and lemon-colored. Gradually beat in powdered sugar. Stir gelatin mixture into beaten yolks. Fold whipped cream into egg mixture. Chill 20 minutes. Cut angel-food cake horizontally into 3 layers. Frost 2 layers with about 1-1/2 cups whipped filling. Sprinkle with ground candy. Assemble cake layers. Frost top and sides with remaining 3 cups whipped cream mixture and top with ground candy. Chill until firm. Refrigerate until serving time. Makes one 10-inch cake.

Variation

4 cups prepared non-dairy whipped topping can be substituted for whipped cream.

Delicious Filled Crepes

FUN SIZE Candies make fun-filled desserts.

Crepes, see below
12 FUN SIZE Candies—MILKY WAY, SNICKERS
   or 3 MUSKEETERS Bars
1 tablespoon butter or margarine

1 tablespoon sugar
tablespoon grated orange peel
cup whipping cream, whipped

Crepes:
1 cup milk
2 eggs
1 tablespoon sugar
1/4 teaspoon salt

1 teaspoon grated orange peel
1 cup flour
Melted butter or margarine

Prepare crepes. Place a bar in center of each crepe, browned side up. Fold 2 opposite sides over candy, then fold remaining 2 sides over. Place folded side down. Just before serving, melt butter in skillet or chafing dish. Arrange filled crepes in skillet. Warm over low heat until light brown, about 5 minutes. Turn carefully; brown second side, 4 to 5 minutes. Fold sugar and orange peel into whipped cream. Serve over crepes. Makes 6 servings.

Crepes:

In a medium bowl, combine milk, eggs, sugar, salt and orange peel. Add flour; beat until smooth. Let batter stand in refrigerator at least 1 hour. For each crepe pour about 3 tablespoons of batter all at once into heated, buttered 6-inch crepe pan or skillet. Rotate pan quickly to spread batter over bottom. Cook until brown on underside and dry on top. Turn out onto a plate. Crepes can be made in advance and refrigerated or frozen, but should be thawed completely. Makes 12 crepes.

Chilled Mocha Soufflé

An elegant finale for any meal.

4 MILKY WAY Bars, cut up
1/4 cup water
1 tablespoon instant coffee powder
1 tablespoon (1 envelope) unflavored gelatin

5 eggs, separated
2 tablespoons sugar
1 cup whipping cream, whipped

In a small saucepan, combine candy, 2 tablespoons of the water and the coffee. Melt over low heat, stirring until smooth. Combine gelatin with remaining 2 tablespoons water. Let stand 3 to 4 minutes. Add gelatin to chocolate mixture. Stir until gelatin dissolves. Cool. Beat egg yolks and sugar until thick and lemon-colored. Add chocolate mixture; blend. Fold in whipped cream. In a medium bowl, beat egg whites until stiff but not dry. Fold 1/3 of egg whites into chocolate mixture. Fold chocolate into remaining egg whites. Spoon into a 1-quart soufflé dish with collar attached, or into 6 to 8 individual molds. Chill 2 to 3 hours. Refrigerate until serving time. Makes 6 to 8 servings.

Molded Rice Pudding

A new flavor twist to an old favorite.

1 cup uncooked rice
1 (3-oz.) pkg. egg custard mix
2 cups milk
1 egg yolk

4 SNICKERS Bars, cut up
1 teaspoon almond extract
Whipped cream for garnish

Oil a 6-cup mold. Cook rice according to package directions. While rice cooks, combine custard mix, milk and egg yolk in a large saucepan. Add candy pieces. Cook custard according to package directions. Pour custard over hot rice. Add almond extract. Let stand 10 minutes, stirring several times. Pour into prepared mold. Chill 4 hours or until firm. Unmold. Garnish with whipped cream. Refrigerate until serving time. Makes 8 servings.

How To Make Molded Rice Pudding

1/Combine custard mix with milk, egg yolk and candy. Cook according to package directions. Pour over hot cooked rice and add almond extract.

2/Chill pudding in mold at least 4 hours. Unmold and garnish with whipped cream and cherries, if desired.

Pears Hélène

Melted chocolate bar sauce makes this famous dessert.

4 MILKY WAY Bars or
   FOREVER YOURS Bars, cut up
1/4 cup whipping cream or half-and-half

1 teaspoon vanilla extract
2 pints vanilla ice cream
6 large canned pear halves, chilled and drained

In a medium saucepan, combine candy and cream or half-and-half. Melt over low heat, stirring until smooth. Stir in vanilla extract. Cut each pint of ice cream lengthwise into thirds. Place in 6 chilled dishes. Top each with a pear half. Serve with chocolate sauce. Makes 6 servings.

Orange-Chocolate Angel Pie

A dreamy pie with a light orange filling.

4 egg whites, room temperature
1/4 teaspoon cream of tartar
1/4 teaspoon salt
1 cup sugar
1 cup "M&M's" Plain Chocolate Candies
Whipped Orange Filling, see below

Additional whipped cream for garnish,
   if desired
Orange slices for garnish, if desired
Chopped "M&M's" Plain Chocolate Candies
   for garnish, if desired

Whipped Orange Filling:
4 egg yolks
1/2 cup sugar
1/4 teaspoon salt

1/4 cup orange juice
1 teaspoon grated orange peel
1 cup (1/2 pint) whipping cream, whipped

Preheat oven to 275°F (135°C). Butter a 9-inch pie pan. Beat egg whites until foamy. Add cream of tartar and salt. Beat until egg whites form soft peaks when beater is lifted. Gradually add sugar 1 tablespoonful at a time. Continue beating until mixture is stiff and glossy. Fold in candies. Spread evenly over bottom and up sides of prepared pie pan forming a shell. Bake about 1 hour or until light brown and surface is dry. Remove from oven. Cool away from drafts. Make Whipped Orange Filling. Spoon filling into shell. Chill at least 6 hours or overnight before serving. Garnish with additional whipped cream and orange slices, if desired, or sprinkle top with chopped candies. Makes 6 to 8 servings.

Whipped Orange Filling:
In a medium saucepan, combine egg yolks, sugar, salt and orange juice. Beat well. Cook over low heat until thickened, stirring constantly. Stir in orange peel. Chill, stirring often until thoroughly cooled. Fold in whipped cream.

Chocolate Dessert Crepes

Do ahead and make quick and easy desserts.

1 cup "M&M's" Plain Chocolate Candies
1-1/2 cups milk
3 eggs, beaten

1 cup flour
1/2 teaspoon salt

In a medium saucepan, combine candies and 1/2 cup of the milk. Melt over low heat, stirring until smooth. Stir in remaining milk. Cool slightly. Stir eggs into chocolate mixture. Beat in flour and salt. Let stand in refrigerator at least 1 hour. Heat a 6-inch crepe pan and brush it with oil. Pour 3 to 4 tablespoons crepe batter into pan and swirl to cover bottom of pan. Cook about 1 minute. Loosen edges, turn and cook other side. Repeat with remaining batter. Chocolate Dessert Crepes can be frozen, tightly wrapped in aluminum foil. Defrost and use at room temperature. Makes about 16 crepes.

Marmalade Crepes

Add filling and sauce to Chocolate Dessert Crepes in a jiffy.

8 Chocolate Dessert Crepes, see above
1 (8-oz.) carton whipped cream cheese

1/2 cup orange marmalade
Fresh orange peel strips, if desired

Heat oven to 400°F (205°C). Spread entire surface of each crepe with about 2-1/2 tablespoons whipped cream cheese. Roll up and place seam side up, side by side, in an oven-proof baking dish. Spoon marmalade down center of crepes. Bake in upper third of oven 5 minutes. Serve hot. Garnish with orange peel strips, if desired. Makes 8 crepes.

Mocha Pots de Crème

This unforgettable dessert has a special deep chocolate flavor.

1-1/4 cups half-and-half
3 3 MUSKETEERS Bars, cut up
1 tablespoon instant coffee powder
3 egg yolks

1 teaspoon vanilla extract
1/8 teaspoon salt
Whipping cream, whipped, if desired

Preheat oven to 325°F (165°C). In a medium saucepan, combine half-and-half, candy and coffee. Melt over low heat, stirring until smooth. In a medium bowl beat together egg yolks, vanilla and salt. Gradually add candy mixture to egg yolk mixture, beating constantly. Pour into 4 to 6 petits pots or small custard cups. Place cups in a pan of hot water. Bake 25 to 35 minutes or until knife inserted near center comes out clean. Chill. To serve, top with a dollop of whipped cream, if desired. Makes 4 to 6 servings.

Orangy Peach Caramel Flan

Pretty as a picture and as good to eat.

1 (11-oz.) pkg. pie crust mix
1/4 cup sugar
1 egg yolk
2 tablespoons water
3 MARATHON Bars, cut up

1/4 cup orange juice
1 tablespoon grated orange peel
1 (1-lb. 13-oz.) can sliced
  cling peaches, well-drained
1 MUNCH Peanut Bar, chopped

Preheat oven to 375°F (190°C). In a medium bowl, combine pie crust mix and sugar. In a small bowl, beat together egg yolk and water. Add to mix. Stir with fork until particles are moistened. Press into a flat round. On a lightly floured surface, roll out into a circle 1 inch larger than a 9-inch flan pan with removable bottom. Press dough over bottom and up sides of pan. Bake 10 minutes. Meanwhile, in a small saucepan, combine candy and orange juice. Melt over low heat, stirring until smooth. Stir in orange peel. Arrange peach slices in baked pastry-lined pan. Drizzle candy mixture over peaches. Return to oven. Bake 25 minutes or until filling bubbles slightly and crust is done. Sprinkle with chopped peanut bar. Cool. Remove rim of pan before serving. Makes 6 to 8 servings.

Mandarin Orange Roll

A half-day production cut to minutes.

1 (10-oz.) pkg. frozen patty shells
1 (3-oz.) pkg. cream cheese, room temperature
1 tablespoon grated orange peel
1 teaspoon butter or margarine, melted

4 SNICKERS Bars, thinly sliced
1 (11-oz.) can mandarin orange segments,
  well-drained
Powdered sugar

Let patty shells stand at room temperature 1 hour. In a small bowl, beat cream cheese until smooth. Stir in orange peel, set aside. Preheat oven to 375°F (190°C). Arrange patty shells with edges overlapping on a lightly floured surface. Roll out into a 10" x 18" rectangle. Spread cream cheese mixture over 2/3 of dough, starting from the narrow end. Spread remaining dough with melted butter or margarine. Arrange sliced candy and orange segments on cream cheese mixture. Roll up pastry beginning at candy end. Tuck ends under to seal. Place on ungreased baking sheet. Bake 30 to 35 minutes or until pastry is crisp and light brown. Cool on wire rack. Sprinkle with powdered sugar. Slice and serve slightly warm. Makes 6 to 8 servings.

Sprinkle chopped MARS Almond Bars over hot, cooked pudding; you'll love the nutty nougat topping.

Chocolate Torte

An impressive torte of layered pound cake, apricot preserves and rich chocolate.

1 Chocolate Pound Cake, page 40
1 (8-oz.) pkg. "M&M's" Plain Chocolate
   Candies

3 tablespoons coffee
1/2 cup dairy sour cream
3 tablespoons apricot preserves

Place pound cake in freezer for 1 hour. Trim top and side crusts from cake to form straight edges. Cut horizontally into 4 equal layers. Reserve 12 candies for garnish. In a small saucepan, combine remaining candies with coffee. Melt over low heat, stirring until smooth. Cool slightly. Stir in sour cream. Spread about 1/4 cup chocolate mixture on 1 layer of cake. Top with second layer; spread with preserves. Top with third layer; spread with about 1/4 cup chocolate mixture. Top with remaining cake layer. Spread remaining chocolate mixture on top and sides of cake. Garnish with reserved candies. Refrigerate 8 hours or overnight. Makes 12 servings.

Cream Puff Crown

Add candles for an unusually elegant birthday dessert.

1 cup water
1/2 cup butter or margarine
1/4 teaspoon salt
1 cup sifted flour

4 eggs
Chocolate Almond Cream, see below
Powdered sugar for garnish
Whipped Cream, if desired

Chocolate Almond Cream:
8 MARS Almond Bars, cut up
1/3 cup half-and-half
Pinch of salt

1 teaspoon vanilla extract
1 teaspoon brandy extract
1 cup (1/2 pint) whipping cream, whipped

Preheat oven to 400°F (205°C). In a medium saucepan, combine water, butter or margarine and salt. Heat to boiling and reduce heat. Add flour all at once. Stir vigorously until mixture leaves sides of pan and forms a soft ball. Remove from heat. Beat in eggs one at a time, beating after each addition until mixture is smooth and shiny. Cool about 15 minutes. Mark an 8-inch circle on a baking sheet lined with aluminum foil. Spoon cream puff mixture into 12 mounds on circle, using a scant 1/4 cup for each mound. Bake 40 minutes or until puffed, browned and crisp. Turn off heat. Let cream puff ring stand in oven 20 to 30 minutes to dry. Prick puffs around inside edge with point of a knife to let steam escape. Cool on wire rack. Make Chocolate Almond Cream. With a fork, cut cream puff ring in half horizontally. Carefully remove top. Remove any soft dough inside. Fill with Chocolate Almond Cream. Replace top. Sprinkle with powdered sugar. Serve with a bowl of whipped cream in center, if desired. Makes 12 servings.

Chocolate Almond Creme:
In a small saucepan, combine candy, half-and-half and salt. Melt over low heat, stirring until smooth. Cool to room temperature. Add vanilla and brandy extract. Fold in whipped cream. Chill about 1 hour.

Napoleons In-A-Hurry

This quick version of a famous dessert has a special sauce.

4 MILKY WAY or FOREVER YOURS Bars,
  cut up
1/2 cup half-and-half

1 (10-oz.) pkg. frozen patty shells
1 (3-1/4-oz.) pkg. vanilla instant pudding and
  pie filling

In a small saucepan, combine candy and half-and-half. Melt over low heat, stirring until smooth. Chill. Let frozen patty shells thaw at room temperature about 1 hour. On a lightly floured surface, place 2 shells, overlapping them slightly. Roll out to make an 8-inch square. Place on ungreased baking sheet. Repeat with remaining shells. Chill about 1 hour. Preheat oven to 400°F (205°C). Bake pastry 10 to 12 minutes, until puffed, browned and crisp. Cool on wire rack. Prepare filling according to package directions. Let stand until thickened. To serve, cut each square of pastry with a serrated knife into 6 pieces. For each serving, place a piece of pastry on a dessert plate, top each with about 1/4 cup filling and then another piece of pastry. Serve with chocolate sauce. Makes 9 servings.

How To Make Cream Puff Crown

1/Draw an 8-inch circle on foil-covered baking sheet. Spoon cream puff mixture into 12 mounds. Use a scant 1/4 cup for each mound.

2/Cool completely and carefully cut puffs in half. Fill with Chocolate Almond Cream. Replace tops and sprinkle with powdered sugar.

Instant Desserts For Unexpected Guests

So you've just found out guests are coming for dinner! Glance through this recipe section for some of the quickest, most delicious desserts you've ever served. Bananas Praline, page 73, is an instant success. Neopolitan Ice Cream Pie, page 74, is a glorious frozen treat. For a super hot and sweet beverage, let your guests try Hot Maple Chocolate, page 73. It'll be ready in a jiffy!

Peach-Glazed Spice Cake

Quick trick for an instant fruit-topped dessert.

1 (16-oz.) can sliced peaches, reserve syrup
1 (9-oz.) pkg. yellow cake mix
1/2 teaspoon ground ginger

1 egg
3 SNICKERS Bars, cut up
1/2 teaspoon ground cinnamon

Preheat oven to 325°F (165°C). Grease and flour a 9-inch, round cake pan. Drain peaches; reserve 3/4 cup syrup. In a medium mixing bowl, combine cake mix and ginger. Add 1/2 cup of the reserved syrup and the egg. Beat with electric mixer on medium speed until smooth, about 2 minutes. Pour into prepared pan. Bake 30 to 35 minutes or until golden brown and wooden pick inserted near center comes out dry. Cool 5 minutes. Remove from pan and place on oven-proof plate. Meanwhile, in a medium saucepan, combine candy, remaining syrup and cinnamon. Melt over low heat, stirring until smooth. Arrange peach slices on top of cake in circular fashion. Pour melted chocolate mixture over peaches. Broil 6 to 8 inches from heat until bubbly, 2 to 3 minutes. Serve warm. Makes 6 to 8 servings.

Peanut Marshmallow Dessert

A beautiful light dessert with a wonderful blend of textures.

2 cups miniature marshmallows
4 MUNCH Peanut Bars, coarsely ground

1 cup whipping cream, whipped

In a medium bowl, stir marshmallows and half the candy crumbs into whipped cream. Chill at least 2 hours. Spoon into 6 dessert glasses. Sprinkle with remaining candy crumbs. Serve very cold. Makes 6 servings.

Chocolate Waffles

You can make these dessert waffles ahead and freeze them.

1 cup "M&M's" Plain Chocolate Candies
1/3 cup milk
2 cups biscuit baking mix

1 cup milk
1 egg

Preheat waffle iron. Brush with oil. In a small saucepan, combine candies and 1/3 cup milk. Melt over low heat, stirring until smooth. In a medium bowl, combine baking mix, 1 cup milk and egg. Stir in chocolate mixture. Pour about 1 cup batter on waffle iron. Cook until steaming stops, 4 to 5 minutes. Makes twelve 4-inch square waffles.

Variation

Serve topped with ice cream or fresh fruit, whipped cream and Creamy Chocolate Sauce, page 102.

Banana Split Crepes

Hot chocolate caramel sauce is the perfect topping for these banana-filled crepes.

8 Chocolate Dessert Crepes, page 63
4 medium bananas
1 tablespoon lemon juice
6 MARATHON Bars, cut in pieces

3/4 cup orange juice
1/2 teaspoon rum extract
1/2 cup chopped nuts
Ice cream, if desired

Prepare Chocolate Dessert Crepes. Cut bananas lengthwise into quarters. Sprinkle with lemon juice. In a medium saucepan, combine candy and orange juice. Melt over low heat, stirring until smooth. Simmer 3 minutes. Remove from heat. Add rum extract. Place 2 banana slices and 1 tablespoon candy mixture in center of each crepe. Fold crepe over filling. Top with another tablespoon candy mixture and about 1-1/2 teaspoons chopped nuts. Serve warm with ice cream if desired. Makes 8 servings.

Black Bottom Pie

Quick and easy pudding pie.

1 cup "M&M's" Plain Chocolate Candies
2 tablespoons milk
1 (9-inch) pie shell, baked

1 (3-3/4-oz.) pkg. instant vanilla pudding and
pie filling mix

Reserve 2 tablespoons candies. In a small saucepan, combine remaining candies with milk. Melt over low heat, stirring until smooth. Pour candy mixture into bottom of pie shell. Place in freezer for 5 minutes. Prepare pie filling according to package directions. Pour over chocolate layer. Let stand until set. Chill. Decorate top with reserved candies. Refrigerate until ready to serve. Makes 6 servings.

How To Make Black Bottom Pie

1/Pour vanilla pudding over chocolate layer. Refrigerate until ready to serve.

2/Just before serving, garnish top of vanilla layer with remaining candies.

Mocha Nut Mousse In Patty Shells

Festive desserts with a special flavor.

1 (10-oz.) pkg. frozen patty shells
6 SNICKERS Bars, cut in pieces
1/3 cup half-and-half
1 teaspoon instant coffee powder

Pinch of salt
1 teaspoon vanilla extract
1 cup (1/2 pint) whipping cream, whipped
Powdered sugar

Bake shells according to directions on package for extra crispness. Cool on wire rack. In a small saucepan, combine candy, half-and-half, coffee and salt. Melt over low heat, stirring until smooth. Remove from heat. Cool to room temperature. Stir in vanilla. Fold whipped cream into chocolate mixture. Refrigerate until serving time. Sprinkle patty shells with powdered sugar. To serve, spoon about 1/2 cup chocolate mixture into each patty shell. Makes 6 servings.

Candy Pudding Cake

Find a surprise chocolate pudding at the bottom of the cake.

1 (9-oz.) pkg. chocolate or yellow cake mix
3 3 MUSKETEERS Bars, thinly sliced
1/2 cup water

1/4 cup light corn syrup or honey
Whipped cream or vanilla ice cream, if desired

Preheat oven to 350°F (175°C). Grease an 8-inch square pan. Prepare cake mix according to package directions. Pour into prepared pan. Arrange sliced candy evenly over cake batter. In a small saucepan, combine water and corn syrup or honey. Heat just until bubbles appear around edge of pan. Pour over cake batter and candy. Bake 30 to 35 minutes or until wooden pick inserted in center comes out dry. Let stand 5 minutes. Spoon out of pan while warm. Serve topped with whipped cream, if desired. Makes 8 or 9 servings.

Zesty Pear Sundae

It's the sauce that makes this a flavor sensation.

12 canned pear halves, chilled
1/2 (12-oz.) pkg. STARBURST Fruit Chews
   (about 35 candies)

2 pints vanilla ice cream, if desired

Drain pears; reserve 1/3 cup liquid. In a small saucepan, combine candies and pear liquid or syrup from canned pears. Heat slowly, stirring until smooth. Chill. Serve pears with sauce over ice cream, if desired. Makes 6 servings.

Bananas Praline

Special enough for a party.

2 tablespoons butter or margarine
1/2 cup orange juice
1/4 cup light brown sugar, firmly packed
1/4 teaspoon ground cinnamon

3 medium bananas, cut in half
  lengthwise, then in thirds
4 MUNCH Peanut Bars
Vanilla ice cream

Melt butter or margarine in chafing dish or skillet. Add orange juice, brown sugar and cinnamon. Heat until bubbling and slightly thickened. Add bananas. Cook just until hot. Sprinkle with chopped candy. Spoon over ice cream. Refrigerate leftovers. Makes 6 servings.

Variation
1 (3-3/4-oz.) package vanilla instant pudding and pie filling can be substituted for the ice cream. Prepare according to package directions and chill. Before serving, fold in 1/2 cup whipping cream, whipped.

Cheesey Crepes In Fruit Sauce

Watch these magically disappear.

12 Chocolate Dessert Crepes, page 63
1 (8-oz.) carton whipped cream cheese
2 (1-11/16-oz.) pkgs. STARBURST Fruit Chews
  (20 to 22 candies)

1/2 cup light corn syrup
1/4 cup water
2 tablespoons butter or margarine

Spread each crepe with about 1-1/2 tablespoons cream cheese. Fold crepes into quarters. Cover and chill until ready to serve. In a small saucepan, combine candies, corn syrup and water. Melt over low heat, stirring until smooth. Keep warm. Melt butter or margarine in chafing dish or skillet. Place crepes in chafing dish or skillet. Heat slowly, turning once. Spoon sauce over crepes and heat several minutes. Serve crepes warm and spoon sauce over top. Makes 6 servings, 2 crepes each.

Hot Maple Chocolate

Perfect for long winter nights.

1/2 cup "M&M's" Plain Chocolate Candies
1/2 cup maple-flavored syrup

1/4 teaspoon maple extract, if desired
2 cups hot milk

Place candies, syrup and maple extract, if desired, in blender container. Add hot milk. Cover container and blend until smooth. Pour into glasses or mugs. Refrigerate any leftovers. Makes 4 servings.

Neapolitan Ice Cream Pie

A triple-treat peanutty pie.

1 (9-inch) pie shell, baked
1/2 cup "M&M's" Plain or Peanut
   Chocolate Candies, chopped

3 pints (3 different flavors) ice cream
Peanutty Chocolate Sauce, see below

Peanutty Chocolate Sauce:
1 cup "M&M's" Peanut Chocolate Candies
1/3 to 1/2 cup half-and-half

1/4 cup light corn syrup
1/8 teaspoon cream of tartar

Chill baked pie shell. Sprinkle about 1/3 of the chopped candies over bottom of pie shell. Spoon ice cream into shell, alternating colors and sprinkling remaining chopped candies between ice cream layers. Store in freezer until ready to serve. Serve with Peanutty Chocolate Sauce. Makes 6 to 8 servings.

Peanutty Chocolate Sauce:
In a small saucepan, combine candies, 1/4 cup of the half-and-half, the corn syrup and cream of tartar. Melt over low heat, stirring until smooth. Chill. Add remaining half-and-half to thin sauce to desired consistency. Serve over pie. Makes about 1-1/4 cups sauce.

Nutty Sweet Potato Pie

A surprising new flavor combination.

3 SNICKERS Bars, cut in pieces
1/2 cup evaporated milk
1 cup cooked mashed sweet potato
1 egg, beaten
1/2 cup sugar

1 teaspoon pumpkin pie spice
1 teaspoon salt
1 (9-inch) unbaked pie shell
Whipped topping, if desired

Preheat oven to 350°F (175°C). In a medium saucepan, combine candy and 1/4 cup evaporated milk. Melt over low heat, stirring until smooth. Remove from heat. In a medium bowl, combine sweet potato, remaining 1/4 cup evaporated milk, beaten egg, sugar, pumpkin pie spice and salt. Pour chocolate mixture into sweet potato mixture; mix well. Pour into unbaked pie shell. Bake about 30 minutes or until knife inserted into center comes out clean. Serve with whipped topping, if desired. Makes 6 to 8 servings.

Frozen desserts taste better if allowed to mellow in the refrigerator 20 minutes before serving.

Peanut Topped Crème Brûlée

Traditional elegance made easy.

1 (4-1/2-oz.) pkg. egg custard mix
1-1/2 cups milk

1-1/2 cups half-and-half
2 MUNCH Peanut Bars, chopped

Make custard mix according to package directions, using 1-1/2 cups milk and 1-1/2 cups half-and-half. Pour into six 6-ounce custard or soufflé cups. Chill. Just before serving, sprinkle chopped candy evenly over top of custards. Place chopped ice in a 13" x 9" pan. Arrange cups in bed of chopped ice. Broil about 4 inches from heat, until candy starts to melt and brown, 4 to 5 minutes. Serve immediately. Refrigerate leftovers. Makes 6 servings.

How To Make Peanut Topped Crème Brûlée

1/Just before serving, sprinkle chopped candies evenly over top of each custard. Arrange cups in a bed of chopped ice in a baking pan.

2/Broil about 4 inches from heat just until candy starts to melt and brown. Serve at once. Custard will still be chilled with crunchy melted topping.

Do Ahead—Take From Freezer Or Refrigerator

A few hours of preparation today will give you a freezer full of desserts ready for any occasion. Frozen Choco-Almond Mousse, page 79, and Frozen Peach Yogurt Pie, page 82, are favorite treats for both family and guests. If you want to make a festive dessert in the morning so you won't be rushed for dinner, whip up Sweet Cherry Bavarian, page 78, and store in the refrigerator until ready to serve.

Mocha Mousse

A special after-dinner coffee treat.

1 tablespoon (1 envelope) unflavored gelatin
1/4 cup cold water
1 (about 3-5/8-oz.) pkg. vanilla pudding
   and pie filling (not instant)
2 cups milk
1 (1-lb.) pkg. "M&M's" Plain Chocolate
   Candies

2 tablespoons instant coffee
1/2 teaspoon rum extract
1-1/2 cups whipping cream, whipped
Additional whipped cream
Whole strawberries for garnish

In a small bowl, combine gelatin with cold water. Let stand 3 to 5 minutes. In a saucepan, combine pudding mix, milk and candies. Cook, stirring constantly, until mixture boils. Remove from heat. Add softened gelatin. Stir until candies and gelatin are melted. Stir in coffee and rum extract. Chill until mixture begins to set. Fold the whipped cream into the chocolate mixture. Pour into a 2-quart mold. Chill until firm. Refrigerate until serving time. Unmold onto platter. Garnish with additional whipped cream and strawberries. Makes 10 to 12 servings.

Chocolate Crunch Cheesecake

Cheesecake is everyone's favorite. This one has a special flavor.

24 shortbread cookies
1/4 cup butter or margarine, melted
1 tablespoon water
1/2 cup "M&M's" Peanut or Plain
   Chocolate Candies, finely chopped
2 (8-oz.) pkgs. cream cheese,
   room temperature
1-1/4 cups milk

1/4 cup sugar
1 (3-3/4-oz.) pkg. vanilla instant pudding
   and pie filling
2 tablespoons lemon juice
1 teaspoon grated lemon peel
1 teaspoon vanilla extract
1/4 cup "M&M's" Peanut or Plain
     Chocolate Candies, coarsely chopped

Crush cookies to make fine crumbs. Butter a 9-inch springform pan. In a medium bowl, combine 1-1/2 cups cookie crumbs and butter or margarine; mix thoroughly. Sprinkle with water; mix. Stir in finely chopped candies. Press crumb mixture evenly over bottom and 1-1/4 inches up sides of prepared pan. Chill. In a medium bowl, beat cream cheese, 1/4 cup of the milk and the sugar until smooth. Add pudding mix and remaining 1 cup milk. Beat slowly until mixture begins to set, about 1 minute. Stir in lemon juice, lemon peel and vanilla. Pour into crust. Refrigerate until serving time. Sprinkle with coarsely chopped candies just before serving. Makes 12 to 16 servings.

Rum Chocolate Tarts

A dainty do-ahead.

1 egg yolk
2 tablespoons sugar

Rum-Chocolate Filling:
2 egg yolks
2 tablespoons cornstarch
1-1/4 cups milk

1 (about 11-oz.) pkg. pie crust mix
Rum Chocolate Filling, see below

4 MARS Almond Bars, cut in pieces
1 teaspoon rum extract

Preheat oven to 400°F (205°C). In a small bowl, beat egg yolk and sugar. Add pie crust mix. Blend to make a soft dough. Divide dough into 8 portions. Press 1 portion into each of eight 4-inch tart pans. Chill 1 hour. Prepare Rum-Chocolate Filling. Bake tart shells 15 minutes or until golden brown. Cool on wire rack. Fill baked tart shells with Rum-Chocolate Filling. Chill until firm, about 2 hours. Refrigerate until ready to serve. Makes 8 tarts.

Rum-Chocolate Filling:
Beat egg yolks in a small bowl. In a saucepan, blend cornstarch with milk. Add candy pieces. Cook over low heat, stirring constantly, until mixture thickens and bubbles, about 2 minutes. Remove from heat. Gradually beat about 1/2 cup hot mixture into egg yolks. Stir back into saucepan. Cook and stir 1 minute. Cool. Add rum extract.

Sweet Cherry Bavarian

A dessert with old-world elegance and new-world ease.

1 (1-lb.) can pitted dark sweet cherries
1 tablespoon (1 envelope) unflavored gelatin
1 cup milk
4 3 MUSKETEERS Bars, cut in pieces
1/2 teaspoon brandy extract

2 (1-3/4-oz.) envelopes whipped
    topping mix
9 to 12 ladyfingers, split, or 18 to 24
    curled sugar cookies
Mystery Chocolate Sauce, page 104

Drain cherries, reserve 1/2 cup syrup. Chop cherries coarsely. In a medium saucepan, combine gelatin and milk. Let stand 3 to 5 minutes. Add candy; melt over low heat. Stir constantly until candy and gelatin are dissolved and smooth. Add reserved cherry syrup and brandy extract. Remove from heat and chill until mixture begins to set. Prepare topping mix according to package directions. Whip gelatin mixture and fold into topping. Fold in chopped cherries. Chill until mixture mounds. Spoon a small amount of gelatin mixture into each of 6 to 8 chilled stemmed glasses. Stand 3 split ladyfingers or cookies upright around edge of each glass. Spoon in remaining gelatin mixture. Refrigerate until ready to serve. Serve with Mystery Chocolate Sauce. Makes 6 to 8 servings.

How To Make Sweet Cherry Bavarian

1/Pour chocolate-cherry syrup mixture over topping and fold in gently. Fold in chopped cherries.

2/Spoon a small amount of chocolate-cherry mixture into each glass. Stand split lady fingers or cookies upright around edge of each glass. Add remaining mixture. Refrigerate until ready to serve.

Frozen Choco-Almond Mousse

Almond and milk chocolate from the candy bar add heavenly flavor.

4 MARS Almond Bars, cut in pieces
1/4 cup milk
1/2 teaspoon rum or brandy extract

1 teaspoon vanilla extract
Pinch of salt
1 cup (1/2 pint) whipping cream, whipped

Line 6 muffin cups with fluted paper or foil baking cups. In a small saucepan, combine candy and milk. Melt over low heat, stirring until smooth. Remove from heat. Cool. Stir in rum or brandy extract, vanilla and salt. Gently fold sauce into whipped cream. Do not overmix. Spoon into prepared muffin pans. Freeze until serving time. Makes 6 servings.

Almond Chocolate Ice Cream

Old-fashioned homemade ice cream with a super chocolate-almond flavor.

12 MARS Almond Bars, cut in pieces
2 cups whipping cream
2 eggs

1/3 cup sugar
1/4 teaspoon salt

In a medium saucepan, melt candy with 1/2 cup cream over low heat, stirring until smooth. Cool slightly. Stir in remaining cream. In a small bowl, beat eggs until light and lemon-colored. Add sugar and salt gradually; continue beating until very thick. Beat in chocolate mixture. Chill in refrigerator about 1 hour. Pour into ice cream freezer and follow manufacturer's directions for making ice cream. Makes 1 quart.

Velvet Pie Supreme

A melt-in-your mouth dessert.

2 tablespoons (2 envelopes) unflavored
   gelatin
3/4 cup cold water
4 3 MUSKETEERS Bars, chopped
1 qt. vanilla ice cream

1 tablespoon grated orange peel
1 (9-inch) baked pie shell
Whipped cream, if desired
Candied orange peel, if desired

In a large saucepan, combine gelatin and cold water. Let stand 3 to 4 minutes. Add candy. Melt over low heat, stirring until smooth. Add ice cream and grated orange peel. Stir until ice cream is melted. Place over bowl partly filled with ice and cold water. Stir occasionally until thickened. Pour into prepared pastry shell. Chill 3 hours or until firm. Garnish with puffs of whipped cream and candied orange peel, if desired. Refrigerate until ready to serve. Makes 6 to 8 servings.

Orange Blossom Trifle

It tastes even better the next day.

4 MILKY WAY Bars, cut in pieces
1/2 cup half-and-half
1 (10-3/4-oz.) pound cake
1/3 cup thick raspberry preserves
1/2 cup orange juice

1/2 teaspoon rum or brandy extract
1 cup whipping cream, whipped
Additional whipped cream, if desired
Whole raspberries, if desired

In a small saucepan, combine candy and half-and-half. Melt over low heat, stirring until smooth. Cool to room temperature. Trim crusts from cake. Cut into 24 crosswise slices. Spread half the slices with raspberry preserves and top with remaining slices. Cut 2 portions of filled cake into 3 lengthwise fingers. Set aside for top of dessert. Cover bottom of a 6-cup glass serving dish with half the filled cake portions. Combine orange juice and rum or brandy extract. Drizzle about half the juice-extract mixture over cake, allowing it to absorb into cake. Fold candy mixture unevenly into whipped cream giving a marbled appearance. Spoon half the candy mixture over cake layer. Repeat with remaining cake portions, orange juice mixture and candy mixture. Arrange cake fingers on top. Cover and chill several hours or overnight. If desired, decorate with whipped cream and whole raspberries. Refrigerate until serving time. Serve with whipped cream, if desired. Makes 8 to 10 servings.

Elegant Coffee Charlotte

Special enough for guests.

1 (3-oz.) pkg. ladyfingers (1 dozen)
1 cup "M&M's" Plain Chocolate Candies
1/4 cup water
1/4 cup sugar
1 tablespoon (1 envelope) unflavored
   gelatin
1/4 teaspoon salt

1-1/2 cups milk
3 eggs, separated
2 tablespoons instant coffee
1/4 cup sugar
Whipped cream, if desired
Additional "M&M's" Plain Chocolate
   Candies, if desired

Line a 9" x 5" loaf pan with aluminum foil. Split ladyfingers in half lengthwise. Stand 8 ladyfingers upright on either side of pan. Line bottom of pan with remaining 8 fingers. Combine candies and water in a small saucepan. Melt over low heat, stirring until smooth. Set aside. In a medium saucepan, combine 1/4 cup sugar, gelatin and salt. Beat in milk and egg yolks. Cook over low heat, stirring constantly, until mixture coats the spoon. Add 1/2 cup custard mixture to the chocolate mixture; mix well. Remove from heat and chill. Add instant coffee to remaining custard mixture. Stir until coffee is dissolved. Chill until mixture begins to set. In a small bowl, beat egg whites until they form soft peaks when beater is lifted. Gradually add 1/4 cup sugar and continue beating until stiff and glossy. Whip coffee mixture until smooth. Fold beaten egg whites into coffee mixture. Spoon into prepared pan. Chill until partially set. Spoon chocolate mixture over coffee layer. Chill until set. Refrigerate until serving time. Garnish with whipped cream and additional candies if desired. Makes 8 servings.

Frozen Peach Yogurt Pie

A refreshing tangy peach flavor.

1 tablespoon (1 envelope) unflavored
  gelatin
3 tablespoons water
1/2 cup milk
2 eggs
1/4 cup light brown sugar,
  firmly packed

2 (8-oz.) cartons peach yogurt
3 MUNCH Peanut Bars, crushed
1 (9-inch) graham cracker crust
Whipped topping, if desired
Sliced peaches, if desired

In a small saucepan, combine gelatin and water. Let stand 3 minutes. Add milk and warm over low heat. Stir occasionally until gelatin dissolves. Remove from heat. Cool slightly. Beat eggs with electric mixer until thick and lemon-colored. Gradually beat in brown sugar and continue beating until very thick. Stir in gelatin mixture, yogurt and crushed candy. Chill about 30 minutes or until slightly thickened. Pour into pie crust. Freeze until firm. Let stand 30 minutes in refrigerator before serving. Garnish with whipped topping and peaches, if desired. Makes 6 to 8 servings.

Praline Mousse With Poached Peaches

A favorite flavor combination from the Old South.

1 cup water
1 tablespoon (1 envelope) unflavored gelatin
1/4 teaspoon salt
2 eggs, separated
1/4 cup sugar
1 teaspoon lemon juice

1/2 cup whipping cream, whipped
3 MUNCH Peanut Bars, finely chopped
6 Poached Peaches, see below, or
  12 well-drained canned peach halves
Whipped cream, if desired

Poached Peaches:
1-1/2 cups sugar
1-1/2 cups water

1/2 lemon, thinly sliced
6 fresh peaches, halved, peeled and pitted

In a medium saucepan, combine water, gelatin, salt, egg yolks and 2 tablespoons of the sugar. Cook over low heat, stirring constantly, until mixture coats the spoon. Chill until mixture begins to thicken. Stir in lemon juice. In a small bowl, beat egg whites until they form soft peaks. Add remaining 2 tablespoons sugar gradually and continue beating until stiff and glossy. Fold into cooled gelatin mixture. Fold in whipped cream and 2/3 of the chopped candy. Chill until praline mixture mounds. For each dessert, fill chilled stemmed dessert glasses 1/3 full. Top with a well-drained peach half. Top with praline mixture, leaving space for a second peach half. Sprinkle with chopped candy. Repeat process. Chill several hours. Refrigerate until ready to serve. If desired, top with additional whipped cream before serving. Makes 6 servings.

Poached Peaches:
In a medium saucepan, combine sugar, water and lemon. Heat to a boil. Add peach halves to boiling mixture and reduce heat. Simmer 5 to 7 minutes. Remove from heat and chill peach halves in syrup.

Angelic Dessert

Use a packaged cake mix or buy an angel-food cake for this easy but very elegant dessert.

10 MILKY WAY Bars
1 (10-in.) angel-food cake, day-old
1-1/2 tablespoons (1-1/2 envelopes)
    unflavored gelatin

1/4 cup cold water
1 tablespoon vanilla extract
3 cups whipping cream

Freeze one whole candy bar. Cut remaining bars into pieces. Slice a 1-inch layer from top of cake. Remove and reserve layer. Scoop out a ring to make a channel in top of remaining cake, leaving a 1-inch rim on bottom and sides. Discard scooped out cake crumbs. Sprinkle gelatin over cold water; let stand until softened. In a small saucepan, combine candy pieces with vanilla and 1/4 cup cream. Melt over low heat, stirring until smooth. Stir in softened gelatin; stir until gelatin dissolves. Cool slightly. In a large bowl, whip remaining cream until stiff. Fold chocolate mixture into whipped cream. Chill 30 minutes. Spoon about 5 cups of the whipped cream mixture into channel in angel-food cake. Replace top layer of cake. Frost top and sides with remaining whipped cream mixture. Cut frozen candy bar into coarse crumbs. Sprinkle over top of cake. Chill until set. Refrigerate until serving time. Makes 12 to 16 servings.

How To Make
Praline Mousse With Poached Peaches

1/Sprinkle whipped cream mixture with 2/3 of the finely chopped candies. Fold in gently. Chill until mixture mounds.

2/Fill each stemmed glass 1/3 full. Top with a well-drained peach half. Spoon mixture over peach and top with a second peach half. Garnish with whipped cream and sprinkle with remaining chopped candies. Refrigerate until ready to serve.

Mahogany Pie

Serve this delicious mocha pie when you need a dramatic finale.

6 MILKY WAY Bars
1/4 cup milk
1 tablespoon instant coffee

1 qt. vanilla ice cream, slightly softened
1 (9-inch) baked pie shell

Chop 4 of the candy bars into small pieces. In a medium saucepan, combine chopped candy, milk and instant coffee. Melt over low heat, stirring until smooth. Remove from heat and cool slightly at room temperature. In a large bowl, gradually beat chocolate mixture into ice cream. Spoon into baked pie crust. Freeze until firm, 3 to 4 hours. Remove from freezer and place in refrigerator 20 minutes before serving. Slice remaining 2 candy bars in half horizontally, then in half lengthwise. Arrange candy slices on top of pie in wedge fashion. Refrigerate until ready to serve. Makes 6 to 8 servings.

Coconut Ice Cream Pie

Choose your favorite ice cream for this simple dessert.

1 cup "M&M's" Plain Chocolate Candies
2 tablespoons butter or margarine
2 tablespoons water

2 (3-1/2-oz.) cans flaked coconut
3 pints coffee, strawberry or vanilla ice cream
Peanutty Chocolate Sauce, page 74

Butter a 9-inch pie pan. In a medium saucepan, combine candies, butter or margarine and water. Melt over low heat, stirring until smooth. Add coconut; stir until coconut is evenly coated with chocolate. Press mixture over bottom and up sides of prepared pie pan. Chill until set. Spoon ice cream into pie shell. Freeze. Serve with Peanutty Chocolate Sauce. Makes 6 to 8 servings.

Favorite Caramel Soufflé

A chocolate-peanut beauty!

6 SNICKERS Bars, cut in pieces
6 tablespoons water
1 tablespoon (1 envelope) unflavored
  gelatin

5 eggs, separated
2 tablespoons sugar
1/2 teaspoon salt
1 cup whipping cream, whipped

In a medium saucepan, combine candy with 3 tablespoons of the water. Melt over low heat, stirring until smooth. Combine gelatin and remaining 3 tablespoons water; let stand 3 to 4 minutes. Add gelatin to chocolate mixture and stir until gelatin dissolves. In a medium bowl, beat egg yolks, sugar and salt until thick and lemon-colored. Add chocolate mixture. Fold in whipped cream. In a large bowl, beat egg whites until stiff but not dry. Fold 1/3 of the beaten egg whites into chocolate mixture; fold chocolate mixture into remaining beaten egg whites. Spoon into a 1-quart soufflé dish with collar attached, or 6 to 8 individual molds. Garnish with whipped cream. Refrigerate 2 to 3 hours before serving. Makes 6 to 8 servings.

No-Trick Halloween Treats

You don't have to be a youngster to enjoy Halloween treats! While the members of the younger set are munching their surprise-filled Treasure Puffs, page 86, or admiring Owl Cookies, page 90, you can serve the adults crunchy wedges of Peanut Crumb Pumpkin Pie, page 90.

Rainbow Oat Bars

A moist bar with a surprise fruit-flavored filling.

1 (8-oz.) bag STARBRUST Fruit Chews
1/4 cup light corn syrup
1-1/2 cups flour
1/2 cup light brown sugar, firmly packed
1/2 teaspoon baking powder

1/2 teaspoon salt
1/2 cup butter or margarine
1 cup oats
1 egg, beaten

Preheat oven to 350°F (175°C). Butter an 8-inch square pan. In a small saucepan, combine candies and corn syrup. Melt over low heat, stirring until smooth. In a medium mixing bowl, stir together flour, brown sugar, baking powder and salt. Cut in butter or margarine until mixture resembles fine crumbs. Stir in oats. Reserve 1 cup mixture. Stir egg into remaining mixture until evenly moistened. Press egg mixture over bottom and 1 inch up sides of prepared pan. Pour warm fruit syrup evenly over bottom. Sprinkle with reserved mixture. Bake 20 minutes or until crumbs are light brown. Cool in pan. Makes 25 bars.

Treasure Puffs

Flakey rolls with a yummy chocolate center.

1 3 MUSKETEERS Bar
1 (8-oz.) pkg. refrigerated crescent rolls

1/4 cup butter or margarine, melted

Preheat oven to 375°F (190°C). Cut candy bar into 8 pieces. Separate dough into 8 triangles. Place a piece of candy on each triangle. Roll up, pinching ends of dough to seal. Dip each roll in melted butter or margarine. Place buttered side up in ungreased muffin pan cups. Bake about 10 minutes or until golden brown. Remove from muffin pan to wire rack; cool slightly. Serve warm. Makes 8 rolls.

How To Make Treasure Puffs

1/Place one piece of candy on each triangle of dough and roll up. Pinch the sides of the roll to enclose candy.

2/Dip each roll in melted butter or margarine and place buttered side up in an ungreased muffin pan. Bake until golden brown, about 10 minutes.

Peanutty Date Bread

Chocolate peanut candy gives this bread mix an individual touch.

1 (1-lb. 1-oz.) pkg. date bread mix
3/4 cup chopped "M&M's" Peanut
   Chocolate Candies

Preheat oven to 350°F (175°C). Grease a 9" x 5" loaf pan. Prepare date bread mix according to package directions. Stir in chopped candies. Spoon into prepared loaf pan. Bake about 1 hour or until a wooden pick inserted in center comes out dry. Remove from pan. Cool on wire rack. Makes 1 loaf.

Confetti Bars

Peanuts and crunch in a rich bar cookie.

1 cup flour
1/2 teaspoon baking powder
1/4 teaspoon salt
1/3 cup butter or margarine
1/2 cup brown sugar, firmly packed

1 egg
1 teaspoon vanilla extract
1/2 cup "M&M's" Peanut Chocolate Candies,
   chopped
1/2 cup ready-to-spread vanilla frosting

Preheat oven to 350°F (175°C). Butter a 9-inch square baking pan. Stir together flour, baking powder and salt. In a large bowl, cream butter or margarine and sugar. Add egg and vanilla. Beat until light and fluffy. Add flour mixture gradually. Stir in 1/2 of the chopped candies. Spread batter in an even layer over bottom of prepared baking pan. Bake 18 to 20 minutes. Cool in pan 15 minutes. Turn out. Cool completely on wire rack. Spread with frosting. Sprinkle with remaining candies. Cut into bars about 3" x 1-1/2". Makes 18 bars.

Pirate's Delight

Melt in your mouth cookie bars with a peanut crunch.

1 cup flour
2 tablespoons powdered sugar
1/3 cup butter or margarine
2 eggs
3/4 cup brown sugar, firmly packed

1/4 cup flour
1/4 teaspoon baking powder
1/2 teaspoon vanilla extract
3 MUNCH Peanut Bars, crushed

Preheat oven to 375°F (190°C). In a medium bowl, combine 1 cup flour and powdered sugar. Cut in butter or margarine with a pastry blender until mixture resembles fine crumbs. Press crumb mixture on bottom of 9-inch square baking pan. Bake 10 minutes. Lower heat to 325°F (165°C). In a small mixing bowl, beat eggs, brown sugar, 1/4 cup flour, baking powder and vanilla. Stir in crushed candy. Pour mixture over crumb layer in pan. Bake 20 minutes until brown. Cool in pan on wire rack. Cut into 1" x 3" bars. Makes about 18 bars.

Caramel-Orange Cookie Slices

Chewy caramel-centered orange-flavored cookies.

2 cups flour
2 tablespoons sugar
1 teaspoon salt
3/4 cup butter or margarine
1/2 cup finely chopped pecans

About 1/3 cup orange juice or water
4 MARATHON Bars
1/2 cup thick orange marmalade
White frosting, if desired

Preheat oven to 375°F (190°C). Stir together flour, sugar and salt. Cut butter or margarine into flour mixture until mixture resembles fine crumbs. Stir in pecans. Add orange juice or water, a small amount at a time, and mix until particles just hold together. Press dough together. Divide into 4 equal portions. On a lightly floured surface, roll each portion into a rectangle about 1/2 inch longer than candy bar and 3-1/2 inches wide. Place 1 candy bar lengthwise down center of each piece. Spoon 2 tablespoons of orange marmalade evenly over each bar. Fold side edges of dough over marmalade until they meet in center. Place on ungreased baking sheet. Bake 20 minutes or until dough is light brown. Cool on wire rack. While slightly warm, cut each into eight 1-inch slices. Drizzle with white frosting, if desired. Makes 32 slices.

Cobcakes

Cupcakes baked in cornstick pans make a delightful dessert.

1 (about 18.5-oz.) pkg. yellow cake mix
1 (16.5-oz.) can ready-to-spread vanilla
   or milk chocolate frosting

1-1/2 (1-lb.) pkgs. "M&M's" Plain Chocolate
   Candies

Preheat oven to 350°F (175°C). Generously grease and flour cornstick pans. Prepare cake mix according to package directions. Spoon 3 tablespoons of batter into each cornstick mold. Bake about 15 minutes. Cool in pans 5 minutes. Cool completely on wire racks. Frost rounded side of each corn stick with ready-to-spread frosting. To decorate for Indian corn, overlap rows of yellow, brown and orange candies lengthwise on frosted cakes. To decorate for corn on the cob, put 2 green candies at one end of the frosted cake. Make 3 overlapping rows of yellow candies lengthwise on cake. Makes 24 cakes.

Variation

1 (7.2-oz.) package fluffy white frosting mix can be substituted for ready-to-spread frosting.

To make a fun snack, mix equal parts "M&M's" Plain or Peanut Chocolate Candies with sesame sticks, rice cereal, pretzels or small salted crackers.

Caramel-Orange Cookie Slices, top, and Cobcakes.

Owl Cookies

Fun treats for Halloween.

1-1/4 cups "M&M's" Plain Chocolate Candies	2 (12-oz.) pkgs. sugar cookie mix
2 tablespoons milk	72 cashews

In a small saucepan combine 3/4 cup of the candies and milk. Melt over low heat, stirring until smooth. Remove from heat. Prepare cookie mixes according to package directions. Stir melted chocolate into half the dough. Form chocolate dough into two 12-inch long rolls about 1 inch in diameter. Wrap in wax paper or foil. Chill until firm, about 2 hours. Divide plain dough in half. On a well-floured surface, roll each plain half out to a 12" x 6" rectangle. Place a chocolate roll on long edge. Roll up, pressing doughs lightly together so plain dough encases chocolate roll. Repeat with remaining dough. Wrap each roll in wax paper or foil. Chill about 2 hours until firm. Preheat oven to 375°F (190°C). Cut each roll into 1/4-inch slices. Place 2 slices so they are touching on greased baking sheet. In the center of each chocolate circle, place one of the remaining candies for eye. Where the slices touch, place a cashew to form nose. Bake until the plain cookie is lightly browned, 8 to 10 minutes. Cool cookies on baking sheets 2 to 3 minutes. Remove and cool on wire racks. Makes 72 cookies.

Peanut Crumb Pumpkin Pie

Crunchy topping is terrific with velvety pumpkin filling.

2 eggs	1 (13-oz.) can evaporated milk, undiluted
1-1/2 cups canned pumpkin	
3/4 cup sugar	1 (9-inch) unbaked pie shell with high fluted edge
2 teaspoons pumpkin pie spice	
1/2 teaspoon salt	4 MUNCH Peanut Bars, chopped

Preheat oven to 425°F (220°C). In a medium mixing bowl, beat eggs slightly. Add pumpkin, sugar, pumpkin pie spice and salt. Mix well. Gently stir in evaporated milk. Pour into pie shell. Bake 10 minutes. Reduce heat to 350°F (175°C) and continue baking until filling is set, 40 to 45 minutes. About 10 to 15 minutes before end of baking time, sprinkle chopped candy over filling. If a less crunchy topping is desired, sprinkle chopped candy on filling before baking. Cool on wire rack. Makes 6 to 8 servings.

Variation
One (1-lb. 14-oz.) can pumpkin pie mix may be substituted for filling and pumpkin pie spice. Prepare according to package directions.

1/Form chocolate dough into two 12-inch long rolls about 1 inch in diameter. Chill 2 hours. On well-floured surface, roll out each half of plain dough to 12" x 6" square.

2/Place chocolate roll on long edge. Roll and press doughs lightly together so plain dough encases chocolate. Repeat with remaining dough.

How To Make Owl Cookies

3/Wrap combined dough roll in wax paper or foil and chill 2 hours. Cut each roll into slices 1/4 inch thick. Place 2 slices so they touch on prepared baking sheet. In center of each slice press plain candies for eyes.

4/Bake until lightly browned, 8 to 10 minutes. Carefully remove cookies while still warm. Cool on wire racks.

Polka Dot Specials

Some candies crack in baking, adding texture to these cookies.

1 cup shortening
1 cup brown sugar, firmly packed
1/2 cup granulated sugar
2 eggs
2 teaspoons vanilla extract

2-1/4 cups flour
1 teaspoon baking soda
1 teaspoon salt
1-1/2 cups "M&M's" Plain Chocolate Candies

Preheat oven to 375°F (190°C). In a large mixing bowl, cream shortening, brown sugar and granulated sugar. Beat in eggs and vanilla. Beat until light and fluffy. Stir together flour, baking soda and salt. Gradually add flour mixture to creamed mixture, beating well after each addition. Stir in 1/2 cup candies. Drop by teaspoonfuls onto ungreased baking sheet. Decorate tops with remaining candies. Bake 10 minutes or until golden brown. Cool on wire rack. Makes about 48 cookies.

Peanutty Caramel Squares

Everyone will love these chewy caramel bars.

1 cup flour
1/4 teaspoon salt
1/4 teaspoon baking soda
1/3 cup butter or margarine
1/2 cup sugar

4 SNICKERS Bars, chopped
2 tablespoons butter or margarine
2 tablespoons milk
1/2 cup shredded coconut
Few drops almond extract

Preheat oven to 350°F (175°C). Butter a 9-inch square pan. In a mixing bowl, stir together flour, salt and baking soda. In a large bowl, cream 1/3 cup butter or margarine and sugar until light and fluffy. Sprinkle flour mixture over creamed mixture. Stir until crumbly. Reserve 1/2 cup crumbs. Press remaining crumbs on bottom of prepared baking pan. Bake 12 minutes or until light brown. In a small saucepan, combine candy, 2 tablespoons butter or margarine and milk. Melt over low heat, stirring until smooth. Stir in coconut and almond extract. Spread chocolate mixture evenly over baked crumb mixture. Sprinkle reserved crumbs over top. Bake 12 minutes or until crumbs are golden. Cool. Cut into squares. Makes about 16 squares.

To make your own sandwich cookies, cut slices of MILKY WAY or 3 MUSKETEERS Bars and place them between baked refrigerated roll cookies as they come out of the oven.

Hidden Treasure Cookies

Bite into these for a fruit surprise.

2-3/4 cups flour
1 teaspoon baking powder
1/2 teaspoon salt
3/4 cup butter or margarine
1 cup powdered sugar
2 eggs

1 teaspoon vanilla extract
1/3 cup milk
Mincemeat Filling, see below
Raisin Filling, see below
Additional powdered sugar

Mincemeat Filling:
3/4 cup "M&M's" Peanut Chocolate Candies,
   coarsely chopped

3/4 cup prepared mincemeat

Raisin Filling:
3/4 cup "M&M's" Peanut Chocolate Candies,
   coarsely chopped

1/2 cup apricot preserves
1/3 cup chopped seedless raisins

Stir together flour, baking powder and salt. In a large mixing bowl, cream butter or margarine and powdered sugar. Add eggs and vanilla. Beat until light and fluffy. Add flour mixture alternately with milk, stirring until blended. Wrap in foil or plastic wrap and chill. When ready to bake, preheat oven to 350°F (175°C). On a lightly floured surface, roll out half of dough 1/8 inch thick. Cut with a floured 3-inch-round cookie cutter. Repeat with other half of dough. Place a rounded tea-spoonful of desired filling in center of each round. Fold in half and press edges together. Seal by pressing edges with a fork. Make 2 or 3 slits in tops of cookies with a sharp knife. Place on ungreased baking sheets. Bake 12 to 15 minutes or until light brown. Sprinkle with powdered sugar. Cool on wire rack. Makes 42 to 48 cookies.

Mincemeat Filling:
In a medium bowl, combine candies and mincemeat. Makes about 1-1/2 cups filling.

Raisin Filling:
In a medium bowl, combine candies, preserves and raisins. Makes about 1-1/2 cups filling.

Variation

Peek-a-Boo Filled Cookies: Using a 1-inch fluted round cutter, cut center out of half the dough rounds. Place 1 teaspoon of desired filling on each remaining round. Top with a cut-out round. Press edges together. Proceed with above baking instructions.

To make Special Cheesecake Glaze, heat 2 packages (1-11/16-oz.) STARBURST Fruit Chews with 3 tablespoons water in small saucepan, stirring until candy melts. Pour over a prepared 8-inch, round cheesecake. Chill. Arrange mandarin orange slices on top before serving.

Conversation Pieces

They'll never believe you made these delicious main dishes with candy! Keep your recipe a secret and they'll come back again and again for more. Tangy Glazed Ham And Chutney Peaches, below, makes an exotic dinner. For a fashionable luncheon, serve Gado Gado Chicken Salad, page 95, with Tomato Aspic, page 96. Both can be made in the morning and refrigerated until serving time.

Tangy Glazed Ham & Chutney Peaches

Fruity ham glaze with a distinctive flavor.

1 (3-lb.) canned ham
2 (1-11/16-oz.) pkgs. STARBURST Fruit Chews
  (22 candies)

1/4 cup orange juice
Chutney Peaches, see below

Chutney Peaches:
1 (18-oz.) can peach halves
1/2 cup chutney

2 MUNCH Peanut Bars, crushed

Preheat oven to 325°F (165°C). In a small baking dish, heat ham in oven 15 minutes. Meanwhile, in a medium saucepan, combine candies and orange juice. Melt over low heat, stirring until smooth. Spoon sauce over ham at 10-minute intervals during baking. Bake ham a total of 45 minutes. Serve with Chutney Peaches. Makes 8 servings.

Chutney Peaches:
Preheat oven to 350°F (175°C). Place peach halves, cut side up, in a baking dish. Fill each peach half with about 1 tablespoon chutney. Sprinkle each with about 1 tablespoon candy crumbs. Bake 10 minutes. Makes 8 servings.

Gado Gado Chicken Salad

For a perfect summer salad, substitute turkey or tuna for the chicken.

2 cups diced cooked chicken
1 cup chopped celery
1 cup halved seedless green grapes
1/4 cup sliced green onions
3 MUNCH Peanut Bars, crushed

1 teaspoon salt
1/2 cup mayonnaise
1 teaspoon lemon juice
1/2 teaspoon curry powder
Lettuce leaves

In a medium bowl, combine chicken, celery, grapes, onions, candy and salt. In a small bowl, combine mayonnaise, lemon juice and curry powder. Toss chicken mixture and dressing to coat. Refrigerate until serving time. Serve on lettuce leaves. Makes 4 to 6 servings.

Hungarian Beef Stew

You'll love this beef stew with its rich brown gravy.

2 cups sliced onions
2 cloves garlic, minced
2 tablespoons oil
2 lbs. beef, cut in 1-inch cubes
1 (10-3/4-oz.) can beef broth
3 FOREVER YOURS or MILKY WAY
    Bars, chopped

2 teaspoons salt
1/2 teaspoon pepper
1/4 teaspoon dried rosemary
1 lb. mushrooms, sliced
2 tablespoons cornstarch
Hot cooked noodles
Chopped parsley

In a 5-quart saucepan, sauté onion and garlic in oil until onion is soft. Add beef and brown on all sides. Add broth, candy, salt, pepper and rosemary. Reduce heat. Simmer covered, about 1 hour. Uncover and continue cooking 30 minutes. Sprinkle mushrooms with cornstarch. Add to beef mixture. Continue cooking until mixture thickens and mushrooms are tender. Serve with noodles. Garnish with chopped parsley. Makes 8 servings.

Baked Squash With Crunch Topping

A unique side dish!

2 (10-oz.) pkgs. frozen yellow squash, thawed
2 tablespoons butter, melted
1 teaspoon salt

1/4 teaspoon pepper
2 MUNCH Peanut Bars, crushed

Preheat oven to 350°F (175°C). In a 1-quart casserole or baking dish, combine squash, melted butter, salt and pepper. Sprinkle with crushed candy. Bake 20 to 25 minutes or until squash is thoroughly heated. Makes 6 servings.

Tomato Aspic

Try this shimmering tomato mold with tuna or chicken salad.

2 tablespoons (2 envelopes) unflavored gelatin
1/4 cup water
4 cups tomato juice
2 (1-11/16-oz.) pkgs. STARBURST Fruit Chews
    (22 candies)
1/2 teaspoon celery salt

1 teaspoon Worcestershire sauce
4 drops hot pepper sauce
1/3 cup chopped green pepper
1/3 cup sliced green onions
Salad greens
Mayonnaise

Combine gelatin and water. Let stand 3 to 4 minutes. In a medium saucepan, combine 1 cup tomato juice and candies. Melt over low heat, stirring until smooth. Add celery salt, Worcestershire sauce, hot pepper sauce and gelatin mixture. Stir until gelatin melts. Blend in remaining tomato juice, green pepper and green onions. Pour into an oiled 6-cup mold. Chill until firm, 4 to 5 hours. Serve on salad greens with mayonnaise dressing. Makes 6 to 8 servings.

How To Make Tomato Aspic

1/In a saucepan melt candies in 1 cup tomato juice. Add celery salt, Worcestershire sauce and gelatin. Stir constantly until gelatin dissolves. Add remaining ingredients and pour into oiled mold.

2/Chill aspic until very firm, about 4 to 5 hours. Remove from mold by inverting aspic onto a platter. Serve with salad greens and mayonnaise dressing, if desired.

Hacienda Chicken Mole

This recipe has a secret ingredient—chocolate.

2 tablespoons oil
3 lbs. chicken pieces
1/2 cup chopped onion
1 small clove garlic, minced
1 teaspoon chili powder
1/8 teaspoon ground cinnamon
1/8 teaspoon ground cloves
1 tablespoon cornstarch

1 (10-oz.) can tomatoes
1/4 cup chopped canned green chilies, more if
    desired
1 teaspoon salt
1 chicken bouillon cube, crumbled
2 FOREVER YOURS or MILKY WAY
    Bars, chopped

Preheat oven to 325°F (165°C). In a large skillet, heat oil. Brown chicken pieces on both sides. Arrange chicken pieces in a shallow 2-quart baking dish. Add onion and garlic to pan drippings and cook until tender but not brown. Stir in chili powder, cinnamon and cloves. Cook and stir 1 minute. Blend cornstarch with undrained tomatoes. Add tomato mixture, green chilies, salt, bouillon cube and chopped candy to onion mixture. Heat, stirring constantly, until candy is melted. Pour over chicken pieces. Cover tightly and bake about 1 hour until chicken is tender. Spoon sauce over chicken several times during cooking. Remove excess fat from sauce before serving. Makes 4 to 6 servings.

Turkey Croquettes With Tangy Sauce

Leftover turkey made into special fare with a crunchy peanut coating.

2 cups ground cooked turkey
1/2 cup finely chopped celery
2 tablespoons finely chopped onion
1/4 cup fine dry breadcrumbs
2 eggs
1 teaspoon salt
1/2 teaspoon dried tarragon

1/4 teaspoon pepper
1 egg
2 tablespoons milk
1/2 cup flour
4 MUNCH Peanut Bars, crushed
3 tablespoons oil
Tangy Mustard Sauce, see below

Tangy Mustard Sauce:
1/2 cup plum preserves
1 tablespoon prepared mustard

In a medium bowl, combine turkey, celery, onion, breadcrumbs, 2 eggs, salt, tarragon and pepper. Shape into 8 oblong patties about 1/2 inch thick. In a small bowl, beat 1 egg and milk. Coat each patty with egg mixture; shake off excess. Roll in flour. Dip again into egg mixture and roll in crushed candy. In a large skillet, brown patties in oil over medium-low heat. Cook about 6 to 8 minutes on each side. Serve with Tangy Mustard Sauce. Makes 8 servings.

Tangy Mustard Sauce:
In a small saucepan, combine preserves and mustard. Melt over low heat, stirring until smooth.

Polynesian Chicken With Peanut Sauce

Try this exotic sauce for a quick chicken dish.

3 lbs. chicken pieces
2 tablespoons butter or margarine
2 tablespoons water
1/2 teaspoon salt
2 MUNCH Peanut Bars, chopped

1/2 cup light corn syrup
1 tablespoon vinegar
1 tablespoon soy sauce
1/2 teaspoon ground ginger
Hot cooked rice

In a 10-inch skillet, brown chicken pieces in butter or margarine. Add water and salt. Cover and cook over low heat until chicken is tender, about 45 minutes. In a small bowl, combine candy, corn syrup, vinegar, soy sauce and ginger. Pour over chicken. Heat about 5 minutes, spooning sauce over chicken to coat well. Serve chicken and sauce over rice. Makes 4 to 6 servings.

Mexican Sunrise Salad

A layered fruit and vegetable salad with a surprise.

2 oranges, peeled, thinly sliced
2 apples, cored, thinly sliced
1 (1-lb.) can julienne beets, drained;
   reserve 1 tablespoon liquid

2 MUNCH Peanut Bars, crushed
1 cup (1/2 pint) dairy sour cream
1/2 teaspoon dry mustard
1 tablespoon honey

In a 1-quart dish, layer half the orange slices, half the apple slices and half the beets. Sprinkle with half the candy crumbs. Repeat, ending with candy. Combine sour cream, mustard, honey and reserved beet juice. Serve as a dressing with the salad. Makes about 6 servings.

Tart Sweet Beets

These beets burst with flavor.

1 (1-lb.) can sliced beets
1(1-11/16-oz.) pkg. STARBURST Fruit
   Chews (11 candies)

1 tablespoon cornstarch
2 tablespoons vinegar

Drain beets and reserve 1/2 cup beet juice. In a medium saucepan, combine 1/4 cup beet juice and candies. Melt over low heat, stirring until smooth. Combine remaining 1/4 cup beet juice with cornstarch. Add to candy mixture. Stir over medium heat until mixture thickens and begins to boil. Stir in vinegar and beets. Reduce heat and continue cooking 2 minutes. Makes 4 servings.

Lamb Patties With Fruit Sauce

Dress up ground lamb with a tangy sauce.

1 lb. ground lamb
1/4 cup chopped onion
2 tablespoons chopped parsley

1 teaspoon salt
1/4 teaspoon pepper
Fruit Sauce, see below

Fruit Sauce:
1/2 cup chutney
1 (1-11/16-oz.) pkg. STARBURST Fruit
  Chews (11 candies)

1/2 cup plain yogurt

In a medium bowl, combine lamb, onion, parsley, salt and pepper. Shape into 4 patties. In a 10-inch skillet, fry patties 6 to 8 minutes on each side or until done. Serve with Fruit Sauce. Makes 4 servings.

Fruit Sauce:

In a small saucepan, combine chutney and candies. Melt over low heat, stirring until smooth. Remove from heat and stir in yogurt. Makes about 3/4 cup.

Sweet & Tangy Cocktail Meatballs

Serve these warm in a chafing dish.

Sweet & Tangy Sauce, see below
1/2 lb. ground beef
1/2 lb. ground pork
1/4 cup chopped onion
1/4 cup chopped green pepper
1/4 cup dry breadcrumbs

1 egg
1 teaspoon Worcestershire sauce
1 teaspoon salt
1/4 teaspoon pepper
1 tablespoon oil

Sweet & Tangy Sauce:
1-1/2 tablespoons cornstarch
1/2 teaspoon mace
1/2 teaspoon dry mustard

1 (10-3/4-oz.) can beef broth
2 (1-11/16-oz.) pkgs. STARBURST Fruit
  Chews (22 candies)

Prepare Sweet & Tangy Sauce. In a medium bowl, combine beef and pork with remaining ingredients except oil. Shape into 30 meatballs about 1 inch in diameter. In a 10-inch skillet, brown meatballs in oil. Drain. Pour Sweet & Tangy Sauce over meatballs. Simmer uncovered 10 to 15 minutes. Makes 30 meatballs.

Sweet & Tangy Sauce:

In a medium saucepan, combine cornstarch, mace and mustard. Add 1/4 cup beef broth. Stir until smooth. Add remaining broth and candies. Melt over low heat, stirring until smooth and thickened. Makes 1-1/2 cups sauce.

Top It Off

After a Conversation Piece main dish, astonish your guests with a dessert sauce made with some of the same ingredients. Top pound cake or ice cream with Chocolate Almond Sauce, page 102. Frost cookies or your favorite loaf cake with Powdered Sugar Icing, page 102. If you like the blend of chocolate, vanilla and marshmallow, serve Rich Marshmallow Sauce, page 103, over vanilla ice cream.

Orange-Chocolate Frosting

A little orange makes a big difference.

1/2 cup "M&M's" Plain Chocolate Candies	1 teaspoon grated orange peel
2 tablespoons water	2-1/2 cups sifted powdered sugar
1/4 cup butter or margarine	2 tablespoons half-and-half

In a small saucepan, combine candies and water. Melt over low heat, stirring until smooth. Cool to room temperature, stirring several times. Do not allow to set. In a small bowl, cream butter thoroughly. Add orange peel, powdered sugar and half-and-half gradually. Blend thoroughly. Beat in chocolate mixture. Makes 1-3/4 cups frosting.

Chocolate-Almond Sauce

A hint of orange makes this special.

4 MARS Almond Bars, chopped
1/3 cup half-and-half

1 teaspoon grated orange peel or
1/2 teaspoon orange extract

In a medium saucepan, combine chopped candy and half-and-half. Melt over low heat, stirring until smooth. Stir in orange peel or extract. Serve immediately. Refrigerate leftovers. Makes 1 cup sauce.

Creamy Chocolate Sauce

A quick way to make a delicious treat.

4 3 MUSKETEERS Bars, chopped
1/3 cup "M&M's" Plain Chocolate Candies

1/2 cup half-and-half
1 teaspoon vanilla extract

In a small saucepan, combine candies and half-and-half. Melt over low heat, stirring until smooth. Remove from heat. Add vanilla. Serve immediately. Refrigerate leftovers. Makes about 1-1/2 cups sauce.

Powdered Sugar Icing

Traditional frosting to dress up cakes, cookies and breads.

1-1/2 cups sifted powdered sugar
About 2 tablespoons milk or half-and-half

1 tablespoon butter or margarine, softened
1/2 teaspoon vanilla extract

In a medium mixing bowl, beat powdered sugar, 2 tablespoons milk, butter or margarine and vanilla until smooth. Add additional milk for desired spreading consistency. Makes about 1/2 cup frosting.

Quick Frosting: Heat 4 MILKY WAY Bars with 1/4 cup butter until candy melts. Spread over baked 13" x 9" x 2" cake. Sprinkle with coconut.

Rich Marshmallow Sauce

A topping for your favorite ice cream sundae.

2 cups miniature marshmallows
1 cup "M&M's" Plain Chocolate Candies

1 cup half-and-half
1 teaspoon vanilla extract

In a medium saucepan, combine marshmallows, candies and half-and-half. Melt over low heat, stirring until smooth. Remove from heat and add vanilla. Chill. Makes about 2 cups sauce.

How To Make Rich Marshmallow Sauce

1/Measure ingredients for sauce. Combine all except vanilla extract in a saucepan. Constantly stir over low heat until blended.

2/Remove sauce from heat and add vanilla extract. Chill sauce until ready to use. Makes an excellent topping for ice cream.

Magic Dessert Sauce

Keep 'em guessing about this tangy apricot-colored fruit sauce.

2 (1-11/16-oz.) pkgs. STARBURST Fruit Chews
  (22 candies)
1/2 cup light corn syrup

1/4 cup water
2 tablespoons butter or margarine

In a medium saucepan, combine candies, corn syrup, water and butter or margarine. Melt over low heat, stirring until smooth. Serve immediately. Refrigerate leftovers. Makes about 1 cup sauce.

Mystery Chocolate Sauce

Quick-to-make and delicious!

1 cup "M&M's" Plain Chocolate Candies
1/2 cup half-and-half

1/4 cup light corn syrup
1/8 teaspoon cream of tartar

In a small saucepan, combine candies, 1/4 cup of the half-and-half, corn syrup and cream of tartar. Melt over low heat, stirring until smooth. Remove from heat and chill. Add 3 to 4 tablespoons half-and-half to thin to desired consistency. Makes about 1-1/4 cups sauce.

Variation

Peanutty Chocolate Sauce: Substitute "M&M's" Peanut Chocolate Candies for plain chocolate candies.

Make a quick topping for a cake or pie by grating a frozen MILKY WAY or 3 MUSKETEERS Bar on top.

For Kids

It won't be only the kids who make these treats disappear! Chocolate & Ice Cream Tarts, page 107, are a special dessert for any occasion. Easy Hot Chocolate, page 108, will warm up the whole family after a winter outing. And it's the rare guest who will turn down a Brownie Sundae, page 108.

Wonder Cookies

This recipe makes enough for a fund-raising event or party.

2 (1-lb.) boxes brown sugar
4 cups granulated sugar
2 cups (1-lb.) butter or margarine, softened
12 eggs, beaten
1 tablespoon vanilla extract
3 tablespoons baking soda

3 lbs. smooth peanut butter
18 cups rolled oats
1 (1-lb.) bag "M&M's" Plain Chocolate Candies
1 (1-lb.) bag "M&M's" Peanut Chocolate Candies
1 (15-oz.) box raisins

Preheat oven to 350°F (175°C). Grease baking sheets. In a large roasting pan, mix brown and granulated sugars and butter or margarine. Add eggs. Add remaining ingredients in order given, mixing well after each addition. Drop cookie dough onto baking sheets using ice cream scoop or 1/3 cup measuring cup. Flatten slightly. Bake 15 to 20 minutes or until light brown. Makes 66 to 72 cookies.

Circle Pop Cookies

Chocolate sandwich cookies on a stick.

1 cup butter or margarine, softened
1 cup sugar
3 egg yolks
3/4 cup dairy sour cream
1 teaspoon vanilla extract
4 cups flour

1 teaspoon baking soda
1/8 teaspoon salt
4 MILKY WAY or SNICKERS Bars
28 wooden coffee stirrers or craft sticks
"M&M's" Plain Chocolate Candies, optional

Preheat oven to 375°F (190°C). Grease baking sheets. In a large bowl, cream butter or margarine and sugar. Add egg yolks one at a time, beating well after each addition. Stir in sour cream and vanilla. In another bowl, stir together flour, baking soda and salt. Add flour mixture gradually to creamed mixture. Divide dough in half. Using half the dough, drop rounded teaspoonfuls of dough 2 inches apart on baking sheets. Cut each regular-size candy bar into 7 slices. Place 1 slice of candy in center of each ball of dough. Place a wooden stirrer or craft stick in dough to form a handle. Top each with an additional teaspoon of cookie dough. With floured fingertips, pat dough to cover candy. Bake on center rack in oven 15 to 20 minutes. Makes 25 to 30 cookies.

How To Make Circle Pop Cookies

1/Drop dough by teaspoonfuls onto prepared baking sheet. Place one slice of candy in center of each ball of dough. Place wooden craft stick in dough.

2/Top candy and stick with another teaspoonful of dough. With floured fingertips press gently on dough to cover candy slice.

Surprise-Filled Cookie Squares

Fun to make, but more fun to eat!

1 (12-oz.) pkg. sugar or oatmeal cookie mix
1/2 cup "M&M's" Peanut Chocolate Candies,
  chopped

Preheat oven to 375°F (190°C). Reserve 1/2 cup cookie mix. Prepare remaining cookie mix according to package directions. Spread out evenly on ungreased baking sheet to make a 12" x 8" rectangle. If desired, place a piece of wax paper over dough; roll out flat with rolling pin. Sprinkle with chopped candies, pressing down slightly. Sprinkle with reserved cookie mix. Bake 12 to 15 minutes or until done. Cut into 2-inch squares while warm. Remove from baking sheet. Cool on wire rack. Makes about 30 cookie squares.

Chocolate & Ice Cream Tarts

Everybody's favorite: ice cream tarts.

1 (4-oz.) pkg. individual graham cracker
  tart shells
4 FOREVER YOURS or MARS Almond
  Bars, chopped

3 tablespoons half-and-half
1 to 1-1/2 pints ice cream, slightly softened

Freeze tart shells. In a small saucepan, combine candy and half-and-half. Melt over low heat, stirring until smooth. Cool to room temperature. Spoon ice cream into frozen tart shells. Spoon sauce between layers and on top. Freeze until serving time. Remove tart shells from pans. Makes 6 tarts.

Peanut Squares

Stir in ingredients one at a time to make the batter for these cookies.

1 cup "M&M's" Peanut Chocolate Candies
1/4 cup water
1/2 cup butter or margarine
1 cup sugar

2 eggs
1 teaspoon vanilla extract
1 cup flour

Preheat oven to 350°F (175°C). Butter a 9-inch square pan. In a medium saucepan, combine candies and water. Melt over low heat, stirring until smooth. Remove saucepan from heat and stir in butter or margarine until melted. Stir one ingredient at a time into chocolate mixture: sugar, eggs, vanilla and flour. Pour batter into buttered pan. Bake 25 to 30 minutes or until surface is shiny. Cool and cut into squares. Makes 16 squares.

Easy Hot Chocolate

This will quickly become your family's favorite hot chocolate recipe.

1/2 cup "M&M's" Plain Chocolate Candies	Whipped cream
2 cups hot milk	Dash ground nutmeg

Place candies in blender container. Add hot milk. Cover container and blend until smooth. Pour into mugs. Serve topped with whipped cream and a dash of nutmeg. Makes 2 servings.

Variations

Viennese Chocolate: Add 2 teaspoons instant coffee powder to candies. Serve topped with whipped cream and a dash of ground cinnamon.
Hot Orange Chocolate: Add 1/2 teaspoon grated orange peel to candies. Serve topped with whipped cream and slice of orange or additional grated orange peel.
Mexican Chocolate: Add 1/2 teaspoon each ground cinnamon and vanilla extract to candies. Serve topped with whipped cream and a cinnamon stick stirrer.
Island Hot Chocolate: Add 1/2 teaspoon rum extract to candies.

Cereal Square Snacks

An easy chocolate crunch treat for kids of all ages.

4 SNICKERS or MILKY WAY Bars, chopped	4 cups crisp unsweetened cereal: rice cereal,
1/2 cup smooth or chunk-style peanut butter	oat cereal, crisp corn puffs or any
1/4 cup butter or margarine	favorite combination
2 cups miniature marshmallows	

Butter a 9-inch square pan. In a large saucepan, combine candy, peanut butter, butter or margarine and 1 cup marshmallows. Melt over low heat, stirring until smooth. Quickly stir in cereal, then the remaining marshmallows. Pat to an even layer in prepared pan. Let stand at room temperature until set, about 1 hour. Cut into 1-1/2-inch squares. Makes 36 squares.

Brownie Sundae

Serve this chocolate delight for a very special day.

8 FUN SIZE Candies—MILKY WAY, SNICKERS or 3 MUSKETEERS Bars, chopped	1 teaspoon vanilla extract
1/4 cup whipping cream or half-and-half	4 brownies, 2-1/2 inches square
	1 pint vanilla ice cream

In a medium saucepan, combine candy and cream or half-and-half. Melt over low heat, stirring until smooth. Stir in vanilla. Remove from heat. Top each brownie square with a scoop of ice cream. Serve warm chocolate sauce over ice cream. Makes 4 servings.

Fun Center Log Slices   *Photo on page 109.*

A chocolate surprise is baked into these cookies.

3/4 cup butter or margarine, softened
1-1/4 cups sugar
3 eggs
1 teaspoon vanilla extract
4 cups flour
2 teaspoons baking powder

1/2 teaspoon salt
1/4 teaspoon ground allspice
1/2 teaspoon ground cinnamon
6 SNICKERS Bars
Cinnamon or powdered sugar

Preheat oven to 350°F (175°C). Grease a baking sheet. In a large bowl, cream butter or margarine and sugar. Beat in eggs and vanilla until light and fluffy. In another bowl, stir together flour, baking powder, salt, allspice, cinnamon. Mix dry ingredients into creamed mixture with hands. Form dough into a ball. Divide in half. Form each half into a log shape. Flatten into a rectangle. Place 3 candy bars in a line along the long half of each roll. Fold dough over bars. Press edges together. Place seam-side down on prepared baking sheet. Bake 30 minutes. Slice when cool. Sprinkle with cinnamon or powdered sugar. Each roll makes about 25 slices.

"GORP" Power Pac Snack

Quick energy for your lunchbox or on a hike.

1 cup dark raisins
1 cup golden raisins
1 cup snipped dried apricots
1 cup snipped dried apples

1 cup salted almonds
1 cup each "M&M's" Plain and Peanut
    Chocolate Candies

Combine all ingredients and store in a covered container or plastic bag until ready to serve.

No-Bake Peanut Drop Cookies

Easy crunch peanut cookies for kids to make.

1 cup "M&M's" Peanut Chocolate Candies
1/2 cup light corn syrup

2 tablespoons butter or margarine
2 cups rice cereal

In a medium saucepan, combine candies, corn syrup and butter or margarine. Melt over low heat, stirring until smooth. Add cereal. Carefully stir until cereal is evenly coated with chocolate mixture; cool slightly. Drop by heaping tablespoonfuls onto wax paper. Let stand at room temperature until set, about 1-1/2 hours. Makes 24 cookies.

Calico Meringues

Melt-in-your-mouth meringues are as light as air.

2 egg whites
1/8 teaspoon cream of tartar

1/2 cup sugar
3/4 cup "M&M's" Plain Chocolate Candies

Preheat oven to 250°F (120°C). Grease and flour a large baking sheet. In a small bowl, beat egg whites with cream of tartar until soft peaks form when beater is lifted. Add sugar 1 tablespoon at a time. Beat until stiff and glossy. Reserve 24 candies. Fold in remaining candies. Drop mixture by teaspoonfuls onto prepared baking sheet. Top each with 1 candy. Bake 30 minutes, until cookies are firm to the touch but still white. Cool slightly on baking sheet; remove with spatula and cool completely on wire rack. Store in an airtight container. Makes 24 cookies.

How To Make Calico Meringues

1/Beat egg whites and cream of tartar until soft peaks form. Add sugar and beat until stiff. Gently fold in candies.

2/Drop meringues by rounded teaspoonfuls onto prepared baking sheet. Top with one candy. Bake about 30 minutes.

Snowball Cookies

No-bake fun-to-make cookies.

1/3 cup butter or margarine
4 cups miniature marshmallows

5 cups rice cereal
1 cup 'M&M's" Plain Chocolate Candies

In a large saucepan, melt butter or margarine. Add marshmallows. Heat slowly until marshmallows are melted. Add cereal. Stir until cereal is evenly coated. Stir in candies. For each ball, fill a buttered 1-cup measuring cup loosely with mixture and drop onto wax paper. Shape into balls. Let stand at room temperature until set. Makes 20 to 22 balls.

Chocolate Drop Cookies

Crisp chocolate sugar cookies.

4 FOREVER YOURS or MILKY WAY Bars,
  chopped
2 tablespoons milk
1 (18-oz.) pkg. sugar cookie mix

2 tablespoons vegetable shortening
2 eggs
1/2 cup crushed cornflakes

Preheat oven to 375°F (190°C). Grease baking sheets. In a small saucepan, combine candy and milk. Melt over low heat, stirring until smooth. Combine candy mixture, cookie mix, shortening, eggs and cornflakes. Drop by teaspoonfuls onto baking sheets. Bake 10 to 12 minutes. Makes 36 cookies.

Caramel-Chocolate Brownies

These brownies are everybody's favorite.

1 (18-oz.) pkg. sugar cookie mix
1 egg

6 SNICKERS Bars, chopped
2 tablespoons milk

Preheat oven to 350°F (175°C). Lightly butter a 9-inch square pan. Prepare sugar cookie mix according to package directions, adding an additional egg. In a small saucepan, combine candy and milk. Melt over low heat, stirring until smooth. Add to cookie dough and mix well. Spread in prepared pan. Bake 35 to 40 minutes. Cool completely and cut into 2-inch squares. Makes 18 brownies.

Fold chopped "M&M's" Plain or Peanut Chocolate Candies into your favorite drop cookie recipe.

Fun Christmas Food And Decorations

Christmas is the time to spoil your family and friends with extravagant sweets, coffeecakes, breads and desserts. You'll find them all on the following pages. You'll also find delightful cookie recipes, including Santa's Favorite Cookies, page 120, and rum-flavored Chocolate Balls, page 115. Make Christmas morning around the tree perfect with Holiday Almond Twists, page 114. Serve them with mugs full of steaming coffee or hot chocolate.

Mocha Puff Pyramid

For special holiday entertaining.

1/2 cup water
1/4 cup butter or margarine
1/2 cup flour
2 eggs

4 MARS Almond Bars, cut up
1/4 cup hot coffee
1 cup (1/2 pint) whipping cream, whipped

Preheat oven to 400°F (205°C). In a medium saucepan, heat water and butter or margarine to boiling. Add flour all at once. Stir rapidly over heat until mixture forms a ball and follows spoon around pan. Add eggs one at a time. Beat well after each addition until mixture is smooth. Press mixture through a pastry bag or spoon into 18 small mounds 2 inches apart on ungreased baking sheet. Bake 30 minutes or until puffed and brown. Remove from baking sheet. Cool on wire rack. In a small saucepan, combine candy and coffee. Melt over low heat, stirring until smooth. Fold half the melted candy mixture into whipped cream. Split puffs. Fill with chocolate mixture. Pile puffs in a serving dish. Spoon remaining melted candy mixture over top. Makes 18 puffs.

Peanut-Apricot Coffeecake

Coffeecake in minutes with refrigerated rolls and a surprise filling.

2 (8-oz.) pkg. refrigerated crescent dinner
  rolls
2 tablespoons butter or margarine, melted
1/2 cup apricot preserves

1/2 cup "M&M's" Peanut Chocolate Candies,
  chopped
1/2 cup sifted powdered sugar
1-1/2 to 2 teaspoons milk

Preheat oven to 375°F (190°C). Grease a 9-inch, round cake pan. Unroll refrigerated dough. Do not separate into triangles. Press 1 section of dough (4 triangles) over bottom of prepared pan. Brush with melted butter or margarine. On a lightly floured surface, arrange remaining 3 sections in a rectangle, about 11" x 13" and press edges together. Spread dough with apricot preserves. Sprinkle with chopped candies. Roll up dough, beginning at short side. Cut into 9 slices. Arrange slices on dough in pan, cut side down. Brush with remaining melted butter or margarine. Bake 25 minutes or until light brown. Cool in pan 5 minutes. Turn out onto serving plate. Mix powdered sugar with enough milk to make a smooth glaze. Spoon glaze over coffeecake. Makes one 9-inch coffeecake.

Holiday Almond Twists

Tender coffeecake with chocolate-almond filling.

1/2 cup butter or margarine
1/4 cup light brown sugar, firmly packed
1 teaspoon ground cinnamon
1 teaspoon salt
3/4 cup milk
1 pkg. active dry yeast
1/4 cup warm water (110°F, 45°C)
2 eggs
4 to 4-1/2 cups flour

1 cup "M&M's" Plain Chocolate Candies,
  chopped
1/4 cup butter or margarine, softened
1 (12-oz.) can ready-to-use almond filling
1 tablespoon sugar
1 tablespoon half-and-half
Powdered Sugar Icing, page 102
1/2 cup "M&M's" Plain Chocolate Candies

In a large bowl, mix 1/2 cup butter or margarine, brown sugar, cinnamon and salt. In a small saucepan, heat milk to scalding or just below boiling, about 180°F (80°C). Pour scalded milk over brown sugar mixture; stir. Cool to lukewarm. In a cup, combine yeast and warm water. Let stand 3 to 5 minutes. Add yeast mixture, eggs and 2 cups of the flour to milk mixture. Beat until smooth. Add additional flour as needed to make stiff dough. Knead on a lightly floured surface until dough is smooth and elastic. Place dough in a greased bowl; turn once to grease top. Cover and let rise in a warm place until doubled in bulk. Punch down dough and let stand 10 minutes. Cut dough into 4 equal portions. Roll out 2 portions of dough into 14" x 6" rectangles. Sprinkle 1/2 the chopped candies over dough. Press into dough slightly. Spread dough evenly with 1/2 the remaining softened butter or margarine and 1/2 the almond filling. Roll up each piece starting on long side. Press edges together securely. Place on greased baking sheet. Repeat with remaining 2 portions of dough. Let rise until doubled in bulk. Preheat oven to 350°F (175°C). Bake about 25 minutes or until light brown. Cool on wire rack. Combine sugar and half-and-half. Brush over hot bread. When cool, spoon Powdered Sugar Icing into indentations and decorate with whole candies. Makes 2 twists.

Chocolate Balls

Add these to your Christmas cookie assortment.

6 3 MUSKETEERS Bars, chopped
1 (5-1/3-oz.) can evaporated milk (2/3 cup)
2 teaspoons rum extract
3 cups fine dry breadcrumbs

1 cup ground nuts
1/2 teaspoon salt
1/2 cup powdered sugar

In a medium saucepan, combine candy and evaporated milk. Melt over low heat, stirring until smooth. Add extract. In a large mixing bowl, combine breadcrumbs, nuts and salt. Pour chocolate mixture over crumb mixture. Stir with spoon or fork. Shape into balls using 1 tablespoonful of the mixture for each ball. Roll balls in powdered sugar. Let stand on wire rack about 30 minutes to dry. Makes about 48 balls.

How To Make Chocolate Balls

1/Combine breadcrumbs, nuts and salt in a large bowl. Pour melted chocolate mixture over the crumbs. Stir to blend.

2/Shape into balls. Use 1 tablespoon of chocolate mixture for each ball. Roll balls in a small bowl of powdered sugar. Place on a wire rack to dry. Store in an airtight container.

Peanutty Peanut Butter Cookies

Add a surprise to a traditional cookie.

1 (12-oz.) pkg. peanut butter cookie mix
1 cup chopped "M&M's" Peanut Chocolate
   Candies

36 to 40 whole "M&M's" Peanut Chocolate
   Candies

Preheat oven to 350°F (175°C). Lightly grease baking sheets. Prepare cookie mix according to package directions. Add chopped candies. Roll into small balls, using 1 tablespoon dough for each. Place on prepared baking sheets. Top each with 1 peanut candy. Bake 12 to 15 minutes. Makes 36 to 40 cookies.

Mocha Brûlot

A coffee classic with a new twist.

1/3 cup "M&M's" Plain Chocolate Candies
1 (3-inch) strip orange peel
2 cups hot strong coffee

1 teaspoon brandy extract
Whipped cream

Place candies and orange peel in blender container. Add hot coffee and brandy extract. Cover container and blend until smooth. Serve topped with whipped cream. Makes 4 servings.

Orange Marmalade Coffeecake

A large, impressive coffeecake with a delightful filling.

1 loaf frozen bread dough, thawed
6 MUNCH Peanut Bars, coarsely crushed
1/3 cup orange marmalade

2 cups powdered sugar
3 to 4 tablespoons milk

Preheat oven to 350°F (175°C). Grease a baking sheet. On a lightly floured surface, roll out dough to an oval about 15" x 8". Reserve 2 tablespoons of crushed candy. In a small bowl, stir remaining candy with orange marmalade. Spread over half of the dough along the long side; leave about 1 inch at outside edges. Brush edge with water and fold other half over filling. Press along edge to seal. Place on prepared baking sheet. Let rise in a warm place until double in bulk, about 30 to 45 minutes. Bake 35 to 40 minutes or until golden brown. Remove from oven and cool on wire rack. In a medium mixing bowl, stir together powdered sugar and enough milk to make a thick glaze. Spread over cooled cake. Sprinkle with reserved crushed candy. Makes 10 to 12 servings.

Holiday Cake Roll

A traditional Yule log cake.

1 cup flour
1 teaspoon baking powder
1/4 teaspoon salt
3 eggs
2/3 cup sugar
2 tablespoons water
1 teaspoon vanilla extract
1/2 teaspoon rum extract

1/4 cup "M&M's" Plain Chocolate Candies,
  chopped
Powdered Sugar
Filling, see below
Frosting, see below
"M&M's" Plain Chocolate Candies for garnish
Whipped cream, if desired

Filling:

1 cup milk
1 (3-3/4-oz.) pkg. pistachio instant pudding
  and pie filling

1/2 cup whipping cream, whipped

Frosting:

1 cup "M&M's" Plain Chocolate Candies
2 tablespoons water
2 tablespoons light corn syrup

3 tablespoons butter or margarine, softened
1/2 cup sifted powdered sugar

Preheat oven to 375°F (190°C). Grease a 15" x 10" x 1" jelly roll pan. Line pan with wax paper; grease wax paper. Stir together flour, baking powder and salt. In a large mixing bowl, beat eggs until thick and lemon-colored. Add sugar 2 tablespoons at a time. Continue beating until mixture is very thick. Fold in water, vanilla and rum extract. Carefully fold in flour mixture. Fold in chopped candies. Spread batter in prepared pan. Bake 12 to 15 minutes until done and light brown. Loosen edges of cake; turn upside down on a clean towel dusted with powdered sugar. Peel paper from cake and trim off crusts. Roll cake in towel, starting at narrow end. Cool. Prepare Filling. Unroll cake and spread with Filling. Gently reroll without towel. Prepare Frosting. Place roll on a serving plate and spread Frosting evenly over top and sides of roll. Do not frost ends. Chill slightly, then make lengthwise ridges in Frosting with a knife blade or fork so surface resembles bark of a tree. Decorate roll with rows of candies the length of the roll. Garnish around bottom with whipped cream and candies, if desired. Refrigerate until serving time. Makes 8 to 10 servings.

Filling:
Combine milk and pudding mix. Beat slowly with mixer about 1 to 2 minutes until blended and mixture starts to thicken. Fold in whipped cream.

Frosting:
In a small saucepan, combine candies, water and corn syrup. Melt over low heat, stirring until smooth. Cool to room temperature, but do not allow to set. In a small bowl, beat butter or margarine. Gradually beat in powdered sugar until mixture is creamy. Add chocolate mixture about 1/4 at a time. Continue beating until very smooth and a proper spreading consistency.

Chocolate Fruit Cake

The combination of fruit and chocolate is superb.

3/4 cup "M&M's" Plain Chocolate Candies
2 tablespoons milk

1 (1-lb. 1-oz.) pkg. nut bread mix
1 (4-oz.) pkg. chopped candied fruit

Preheat oven to 350°F (175°C). Grease and flour a 9" x 5" loaf pan. In a small saucepan, combine candies and milk. Melt over low heat, stirring until smooth. Prepare bread mix according to package directions. Stir in candies and fruit. Pour batter into prepared pan. Bake about 1 hour or until wooden pick inserted near center of loaf comes out dry. Decorate as desired. Makes one 9" x 5" loaf.

Hot Russian Punch

Serve this at your next holiday brunch.

4 cups tomato juice
2 (1-11/16-oz.) pkgs. STARBURST Fruit
    Chews (22 candies)

1 cup (1/2 pint) dairy sour cream

In a medium saucepan, combine tomato juice and candies. Melt over low heat, stirring until smooth. Serve warm with a dollop of sour cream. Makes 6 servings.

Chocolate & Peanut Popcorn Balls

Everybody's favorite popcorn ball!

8 MARATHON Bars, cut up
3 tablespoons water
1-1/2 cups "M&M's" Peanut Chocolate
    Candies

8 cups (2 qts.) popped popcorn

In a medium saucepan, combine candy and water. Melt over low heat, stirring until smooth. In a large mixing bowl, combine peanut candies and popcorn. Pour melted chocolate over popcorn. Stir quickly to coat evenly. With well-buttered hands, shape about 1 cup of the popcorn mixture into a ball. Place on wax paper to cool. Repeat with remaining popcorn mixture. Makes 8 popcorn balls.

Ginger Christmas Cookies

Good enough to hang on a Christmas tree!

3-1/2 cups flour
1-1/2 teaspoons ground ginger
1-1/2 teaspoons ground cinnamon
1 teaspoon baking soda
1 teaspoon ground cloves
1/2 teaspoon salt
1/2 teaspoon ground cardamom, if desired
3/4 cup butter or margarine, softened

3/4 cup sugar
1 egg
2/3 cup light molasses
1-1/2 teaspoons grated orange peel
Ready-to-spread vanilla frosting
1 (1-lb.) pkg. "M&M's" Plain Chocolate
    Candies

Combine flour, ginger, cinnamon, baking soda, cloves, salt and cardamom, if desired. In a large bowl. cream butter or margarine and sugar. Add egg, molasses and orange peel. Beat until light and fluffy. Beat in flour mixture 1/4 at a time, beating well after each addition. Shape into 3 round flat patties. Wrap patties in foil or plastic wrap. Chill. When ready to bake, preheat oven to 325°F (165°C). On a lightly floured surface, roll dough 1/4 inch thick. Cut into shapes with floured cookie cutters. To hang on Christmas tree, use a metal skewer to make 2 holes side by side 1/4 inch apart at top of unbaked cookies. Place 1 inch apart on ungreased cookie sheets. Bake 12 to 15 minutes or until done. Place cookies on wire racks to cool. Decorate as desired with frosting and candies. Allow frosting to harden. To hang on tree, thread narrow ribbon through holes. Makes 36 to 48 cookies.

Santa's Favorite Cookies

Our favorites too.

3 cups flour
1-1/2 teaspoons baking powder
1/2 teaspoon salt
3/4 cup butter or margarine
1 cup granulated or brown sugar,
    firmly packed

2 eggs
2 teaspoons vanilla extract
1 cup "M&M's" Plain or Peanut Chocolate
    Candies, finely chopped

Preheat oven to 375°F (190°C). Combine flour, baking powder and salt. In a large bowl, cream butter or margarine and sugar. Add eggs and vanilla. Beat until light and fluffy. Stir in flour mixture just until blended. Divide into 2 equal portions. Chill dough slightly. Shape each half into rolls about 8 inches long. Wrap in wax paper or foil and chill. Cut rolls into slices about 1/8 inch thick. Place on ungreased baking sheet. Sprinkle with chopped candies. Bake 6 to 8 minutes or until done. Makes 72 to 80 cookies.

Variation

Commercial refrigerated sugar cookies may be sliced as directed on package label, sprinkled with finely chopped candies and baked as directed on package label.

Spicy Steamed Pudding

Serve chocolate candied fruit pudding for your Christmas dinner finale.

6 **MILKY WAY** Bars, cut up
1/3 cup vegetable shortening
1 (about 18.5-oz.) pkg. spice cake mix

4 eggs
1 (4-oz.) carton candied fruit, chopped
1 tablespoon rum extract
Sauce, see below

Sauce:
1 cup (1/2 pint) French vanilla ice cream

Grease a 1-1/2 quart pudding mold. Place about 5 inches of water and a rack in a large pot. Heat to boiling. In a medium saucepan, combine candy and shortening. Melt over low heat, stirring until smooth. In a large mixing bowl, combine cake mix, chocolate mixture and eggs. Beat until smooth, 2 to 3 minutes. Stir in candied fruit and rum extract. Pour into mold and cover tightly. Place on rack in pot of boiling water. Bring water to a boil and reduce heat. Cover and steam 3 hours. Add water as needed to cover the lower 1/4 of the mold. Serve warm with Sauce. Makes 6 servings.

Sauce:
Let ice cream stand at room temperature 15 to 20 minutes or until melted.

How To Make Spicy Steamed Pudding

1/In a large bowl combine cake mix, chocolate mixture and egg. Beat until smooth. Stir in candied fruit and rum extract. Pour into mold.

2/Steam covered mold according to directions for about 3 hours. Remove from water. Cool slightly and uncover. Invert mold onto a serving dish and carefully remove mold.

Lucia Buns

Updated version of a traditional Scandinavian Christmas roll.

1 (13-3/4-oz.) pkg. hot roll mix
3/4 cup warm water (110°F, 45°C)
4 tablespoons sugar
2 tablespoons butter or margarine, softened
1 egg
1/4 teaspoon ground nutmeg
1/8 teaspoon powdered saffron
1/4 cup "M&M's" Plain Chocolate Candies,
   chopped

1 tablespoon milk
1/2 cup powdered sugar
1-1/2 teaspoons butter
1 tablespoon sugar
1-1/2 teaspoons milk
Additional "M&M's" Plain Chocolate Candies

In a large bowl, combine yeast from package with warm water. Beat in sugar, butter or margarine, egg, nutmeg and saffron. Stir in flour mixture from package. Cover and let rise in warm place until doubled in bulk, about 45 minutes. Knead dough on lightly floured surface until smooth and elastic. Roll into about 12-inch square. Sprinkle evenly with chopped candies and press into dough. Fold dough into thirds to make rectangle about 12" x 4"; press down. Cut dough crosswise into 18 strips. Roll each strip into a 14-inch rope, then cut in half. Shape the two pieces of dough into a bun in this way: Arrange 2 pieces of dough to form an X, then roll each end of dough, all in same direction, to make a circle. Place on greased baking sheet. Let rise until doubled in bulk. Meanwhile, preheat oven to 350°F (175°C). Make indentation with finger or back of 1/4-teaspoon measuring spoon in center of each circle. Bake 15 to 18 minutes or until light brown. Mix 1 tablespoon sugar and milk; brush over top of hot buns. Cool slightly. In a small bowl, beat powdered sugar, butter and milk until smooth. Place a dab of icing in center of each circle and fill with a whole candy. Makes 18 buns.

Variation

Ready-to-spread vanilla frosting can be substituted for icing.

Chocolate Gems

Make these for special gifts.

1 cup graham cracker crumbs
1/4 cup butter or margarine, melted
1 cup "M&M's" Plain Chocolate Candies
1 cup coconut

1 (14-oz.) can sweetened condensed
   (not evaporated) milk
1/2 cup chopped pecans

Preheat oven to 350°F (175°C). Grease a 9-inch square pan. Sprinkle crumbs in bottom of pan. Pour melted butter or margarine over crumbs. Sprinkle candies over crumb mixture. Sprinkle coconut over candies. Pour condensed milk over coconut. Sprinkle pecans over top. Bake 25 to 30 minutes or until golden brown. Cut into 1-inch squares. Makes 18 squares.

Christmas Tree Bread

It tastes as good as it looks.

3/4 cup milk
3/4 cup butter or margarine
1/4 cup brown sugar, firmly packed
1 teaspoon ground cinnamon
1 teaspoon salt
1 package active dry yeast
1/4 cup warm water (110°F, 45°C)
2 eggs
4 to 4-1/2 cups flour

1 cup "M&M's" Peanut Chocolate Candies,
   coarsely chopped
1 (12-oz.) can ready-to-use apricot filling
1 tablespoon sugar
1 tablespoon half-and-half
Powdered Sugar Icing, page 102
Additional "M&M's" Peanut Chocolate
   Candies

In a small saucepan, heat milk to scalding or just below boiling, about 180°F (80°C). In a large bowl, pour milk over 1/2 cup of the butter or margarine, brown sugar, cinnamon and salt; stir. Cool to lukewarm. Combine yeast and warm water and let stand 3 to 5 minutes. Add dissolved yeast, eggs and 2 cups flour to milk mixture; beat until smooth. Add additional flour as needed to make a stiff dough. Knead on lightly floured surface until dough is smooth and elastic. Place in greased bowl; turn once to grease top. Cover and let rise in warm place until doubled in bulk. Punch down dough; let rise 10 minutes. Preheat oven to 350°F (175°C). Grease 2 baking sheets. Cut dough in 2 equal portions. Roll each portion out into an 11-inch square. Sprinkle each with 1/2 the chopped candies. Press into dough slightly. Spread each evenly with 1/2 of the remaining softened butter and apricot filling. Roll up jelly-roll fashion. Pinch edges together to seal. Cut in 1-inch slices. Arrange slices on greased baking sheet in the shape of a tree, using 4 slices for the bottom of the tree and 1 for the trunk. Let rise until doubled in bulk. Bake 25 minutes or until brown. Cool on wire rack. Mix sugar and half-and-half. Brush over bread while warm. When cool, drizzle with Powdered Sugar Icing and decorate with additional candies. Makes 2 coffeecake trees.

Zesty Popcorn Balls

Popcorn balls bursting with flavor.

1 (8-oz.) pkg. STARBURST Fruit Chews
1/4 cup corn syrup

2 tablespoons water
8 cups (2 qts.) popped popcorn

In a medium saucepan, combine candy, corn syrup and water. Melt over low heat, stirring until smooth. When candies are melted, bring mixture to boiling and cook 5 minutes. Cool slightly. Pour over popcorn and stir to coat evenly. With well-buttered hands, shape about 1 cup of the popcorn mixture into a ball. Place on wax paper to cool. Repeat with remaining popcorn mixture. Makes 8 popcorn balls.

Variation

Chocolate Popcorn Balls: Add 1 cup "M&M's" Plain or Peanut Chocolate Candies to popcorn before mixing with candy mixture.

Noël Tortoni

A special Christmas treat.

1 qt. vanilla ice cream
1/4 cup chopped toasted almonds
1/4 cup green maraschino cherries,
   well-drained, chopped
1 teaspoon rum extract
1 teaspoon vanilla extract

1/8 teaspoon gound nutmeg
1/2 cup "M&M's" Plain Chocolate Candies
Whipped cream, if desired
Additional "M&M's" Plain Chocolate Candies,
   if desired

Cut ice cream into large chunks and place in a chilled bowl. Stir until smooth. Stir in almonds, cherries, rum and vanilla extracts and nutmeg. Fold in candies. Spoon into 2-1/2-inch fluted paper or foil baking cups in muffin pans. Freeze. Serve plain or top each with whipped cream and a few additional candies. Makes 8 servings.

Variation

Mixed candied fruit may be substituted for marschino cherries.

How To Make Noël Tortoni

1/Stir softened ice cream until smooth. Add almonds, cherries, extracts and nutmeg. Fold in candies.

2/Spoon ice cream mixture into paper or foil baking cups in a muffin pan. Freeze. Top with whipped cream and candies.

Italian Pastry Shells

Cannoli tubes are narrow metal tubes about 5 inches long and 1 inch in diameter.

Oil for deep-fat frying
1-1/2 cups flour
1/4 cup sugar
1/2 teaspoon salt

1 egg
1 tablespoon shortening
1/4 to 1/3 cup water
Candied Filling, see below

Candied Filling:

2 pounds ricotta cheese
1 cup "M&M's" Plain Chocolate Candies,
  chopped

1 (4-oz.) carton candied fruit, finely chopped
1 cup powdered sugar
1 tablespoon vanilla extract

Fill a 3-quart saucepan with oil to depth of 2 to 3 inches. In a medium bowl, combine flour, sugar and salt. In another medium bowl, beat egg and shortening. Mix in flour mixture. Add water, 1 tablespoon at a time, until dough begins to stick together and form a ball. Turn out onto lightly floured surface and knead 1 to 2 minutes. Let dough rest at least 5 minutes or cover and chill for easier handling. Roll dough on lightly floured surface to 1/8-inch thickness. Cut with 3-inch-round cookie cutter. Roll out into oval with rolling pin. Wrap each oval around a cannoli tube; brush edge with water, pressing dough together. Fry in hot oil for 2 to 3 minutes or until golden brown. Remove from oil and slip shell off tube. Drain on paper towel. Cool completely before filling. Pastry shells can be prepared a day ahead, if desired. Fill with 1/4 cup Candied Filling just before serving. Makes 20 cannoli shells.

Candied Filling:

In a medium bowl, beat ricotta until smooth. Stir in remaining ingredients. Chill at least 30 minutes. Makes 5 cups.

Creative Crafts

With candies and bits and pieces of materials you can create a craft project for every occasion. M&M/MARS Products offer a unique opportunity for decorating and creating remarkable crafts. Their special qualities include:

Flavors—M&M/MARS bars and candies are festive; they're great to take as crafted favors to class parties or to decorate your home for holidays and special occasions.

Colors—The bright colors of "M&M's" Chocolate Candies, the golden hue of MUNCH Peanut Bars, and the gentle pastels of STARBURST Fruit Chews offer an array of fun colors to decorate all crafts.

Edible Attraction—M&M/MARS candies and bars adapt beautifully as edible, ornate centerpieces, place cards, favors or party decorations.

For a colorful table decoration, the Poppy Centerpiece, page 128 is easily assembled. Nothing matches the excitement of a piñata at a children's party. This Halloween, surprise your children with their own Jack-O-Lantern Piñata, page 129. Festive Easter Baskets, page 134, make a traditional basket to fill every spring. Many of these craft projects can be made by children as long as they have adult supervision.

Popcorn Chain

Your favorite popcorn ball recipe
1 (1-lb.) pkg. "M&M's" Plain Chocolate Candies
Clear plastic wrap

1/2-inch wide ribbon for tying balls
Several long ribbon streamers, 1 inch wide
Small pair of scissors

Add "M&M's" Plain Chocolate Candies to your favorite popcorn ball recipe. Form balls about 2-1/2-inches in diameter. Wrap each ball in a square of clear pastic wrap. Gather corners and twist to enclose popcorn ball. If desired, wrap fortune or good wish around popcorn ball. Tie ribbon in bow around twist. Hang one long ribbon streamer in doorway or between two posts. Tie each popcorn ball to hanging streamer with one of the remaining streamers. Tie small pair of scissors to hanging streamer so guests can cut off popcorn balls. Makes 1 chain.

Poppy Centerpiece

12 (7-oz.) plastic coffee cup inserts
Stapler
1 pkg. red tissue paper
1 pkg. green tissue paper

Double-faced transparent tape
12 (11-inch) squares of clear plastic wrap
3 (1-lb.) pkgs. "M&M's" Plain Chocolate
   Candies (6 cups)

Base:

On flat work surface, place 8 plastic cups in a circle with sides touching and narrow ends in center. Staple cups together. Place remaining 4 cups in smaller circle on top—they will fit into the depression created by 8-cup circle. Staple cups to bottom cups.

Poppies:

Cut twelve 10-inch circles from red tissue paper. Put a piece of double-faced tape in bottom of each cup. Insert a tissue circle in each cup so it lines the cup. Crush scraps of red tissue and insert in bottom of each cup. Cut five 7-inch circles from green tissue. Insert in openings between cups around small circle and at top. Pour 1/2 cup candies into center of each plastic square, gather up corners and edges and twist to enclose candies loosely. Fasten twist with piece of tape. Place 1 to 2 pieces of tape in each cup to hold crushed tissue. Insert one candy packet in each cup, pushing in place against tape to fasten. Place centerpiece on table and let guests pick a candy packet for a treat. Makes 1 centerpiece.

Jack-O-Lantern Piñata

1 large round balloon
1 bottle liquid starch
Torn (not cut) newspaper strips,
    about 2-inches wide
Straight pin
Scissors
Masking or strapping tape
34-inch length of light clothesline
1 package orange tissue paper
1/4 package green tissue paper
Rubber cement
Black construction paper
FUN and FUN SIZE Candies—MUNCH Peanut
    Bars, MARS Almond Bars, MILKY WAY,
    SNICKERS and 3 MUSKETEERS Bars and
    "M&M's" Plain and Peanut Chocolate
    Candies (wrapped), plus STARBURST Fruit
    Chews. Reguar size bars can be used if desired.
Clothesline
Blindfold
Children's toy broom or stick about 36 inches long

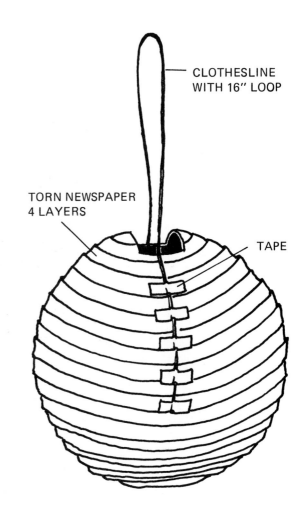

CLOTHESLINE WITH 16" LOOP

TORN NEWSPAPER 4 LAYERS

TAPE

Blow up balloon to 12 or 13 inches and seal it with a knot. Pour starch into small bowl. Dip newspaper strips one at a time into starch. Wipe off excess starch on edge of bowl. Apply strips to balloon so they overlap each other about 1/4 inch and all lay in the same direction. Cover the entire balloon except for a 2" x 2" patch around knot. Apply a second layer of strips in same way, laying them across the first strips. Apply two more layers in same way for a total of 4 layers. This gives the piñata strength. Let dry 3 days before proceeding. Makes 1 piñata.

Decoration:

With straight pin, deflate ballon and remove through opening. If desired, cut opening slightly larger with scissors. Tape clothesline to newspaper shell as in drawing, leaving a 16-inch loop at top for handle. Cut orange tissue paper package crosswise into 3-inch widths. Open each strip; fold in half lengthwise. Cut into folded edge with scissors at 1/4-inch intervals, cutting 1-inch in from fold to make fringe. Repeat with remaining orange tissue and with green tissue papers. Beginning at top, attach green fringed strips to piñata as follows. Brush long uncut edge of folded strip with rubber cement. Apply to newspaper surface around opening in circular fashion with fringed edge up. Overlap rows so only fringes show. After applying 2 to 3 rows of green, change to orange strips and cover remainder of piñata with orange. Let dry. Cut triangular eyes and nose, and a toothy smile from black construction paper. Glue in place. Fill with candies. Suspend piñata with clothesline. Blindfold children one at a time and let them try breaking the piñata with the broom or stick. When the piñata breaks, candy will scatter and the children will scramble.

Candy Cone Ornament

Cardboard
Pencil
Ruler
Red glossy art paper

White glue
1 (8-inch) paper doily
Red crinkle ribbon

Draw a cone as shown in drawing on cardboard with pencil and ruler. Cut out pattern. Place on red paper. Draw around the pattern with a pencil, but use the solid line as a guide for curve. Cut along pencil lines. Place pattern on doily as shown in pattern drawing. Cut doily cone section using broken line as an edge. Roll red piece into a cone, overlapping as indicated on pattern drawing. Fasten with white glue along overlap. Roll doily section into a cone and glue in same manner. After glue dries, insert doily liner in red cone. Punch two holes in cone opposite each other about 1/4 inch from top edge of red cone. Cut 12-inch length of crinkle ribbon. Insert ends of ribbon through holes from outside of cone; tie knot in each end of ribbon. Fill cone with MARS Almond, MILKY WAY, SNICKERS, or 3 MUSKETEERS Bars or STARBURST Fruit Chews, "M&M's" Plain or Peanut Chocolate Candies, and hang on tree. Makes 1 ornament.

Candy Christmas Heart

Glossy red and white paper
Ruler
Pencil
Sissors

Red crinkle ribbon
Paper punch
**FUN SUZE Candies—MILKY WAY, SNICKERS,
3 MUSKETEERS or MARATHON Bars**

Cut one red and one white rectangle, each 3" x 8". Fold in half with right sides out. Draw light pencil line 1 inch from top edge, as in drawing 1. Cut away corners above line to round off. Cut slits 1 inch apart as in drawing 2. Weave the red and white pieces together as in drawing 3. Cut one 16-inch and one 21-inch length of ribbon. Punch hole in heart as shown in drawing 3. Thread 21-inch length of ribbon through hole and tie in a knot, then a bow. Thread remaining piece of ribbon between bow and heart; tie knot in end to form loop. Fill with candies. Hang by loop. Makes 1 ornament.

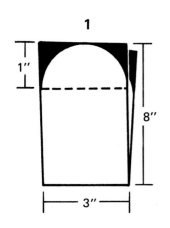

1

1"

8"

3"

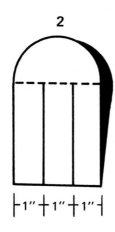

2

1" 1" 1"

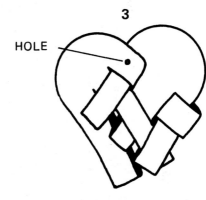

3

HOLE

Candy Christmas Heart

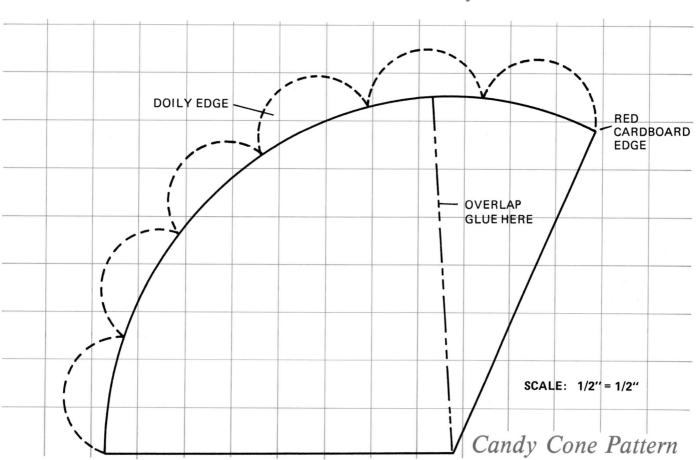

DOILY EDGE

RED CARDBOARD EDGE

OVERLAP GLUE HERE

SCALE: 1/2" = 1/2"

Candy Cone Pattern

Ball Tree Ornament

Clear plastic wrap
1 (1-lb.) pkg. "M&M's" Plain or Peanut
   Chocolate Candies

Crinkly ribbon
Scissors

Tear off 11-inch squares of clear plastic wrap. Pour 1/4 cup "M&M's" Plain Chocolate Candies and 1/4 cup "M&M's" Peanut Chocolate Candies into center of each square. Gather corners and twist to enclose candies tightly. Fasten twist by tying with 30-inch length of crinkly ribbon. Form a loop at top of candy ball for hanging. Tie a 12-inch length of ribbon at base of loop. Curl all ribbon ends with scissors blade. Hang on tree. Makes 1 ornament.

Flocked Christmas Tree

Cardboard
Aluminum foil
5 quarts popped unsalted
   small, white kernel popcorn
2 cups sugar
1 cup light corn syrup
1/2 cup butter or margarine

1/2 cup water
1/8 teaspoon cream of tartar
1 (7.2-oz.) pkg. fluffy white frosting mix
About 1-1/2 cups "M&M's" Peanut
   Chocolate Candies
5-1/2 yards white satin ribbon, about 5-1/6-inch
   wide to make 45 to 50 small bows

Cut an 8-inch circle of cardboard and cover with aluminum foil. Place cardboard on baking sheet. Pour popped corn in large buttered roasting pan. Place in a very low oven (250°F, 120°C). Combine sugar, syrup, butter or margarine, water and cream of tartar in saucepan. Cook over moderate heat until syrup reaches hard-ball stage or until a few drops in very cold water form a ball hard enough to hold its shape. Pour syrup in a very fine stream over popcorn and stir with buttered metal spoon until evenly coated. Quickly spoon popcorn onto foil-covered cardboard. Shape popcorn into a tree about 10-inches tall. Do not pack. An extra pair of hands will help to speed up tree building. Cool tree several hours or overnight. To decorate tree, prepare frosting as directed on package label. *Flock* tree with dabs of frosting and press Chocolate Candies into each dab of frosting. Allow frosting to set. To make bows, cut ribbon into four 1/2-inch lengths. Tie with a single knot in center. Cut end neatly on a slant. Attach bows to tree with pins. Arrange tree on attractive tray or plate and decorate base with evergreen or holly if desired. Makes 1 tree about 10-inches tall.

Spring Flower Cookie Planters

1 (18-oz.) pkg. refrigerated cookie dough
18 wooden craft sticks
White or colored frosting
"M&M's" Plain or Peanut Chocolate
    Candies, as desired
18 small plastic or clay flowerpots

Preheat oven to 350°F (175°C). Slice cookie dough according to package directions. Place half of the cookies on an ungreased baking sheet 4 inches apart. Place end of wooden craft stick in center of each cookie. Top with a second cookie and press gently. Bake 10 to 12 minutes until done and light brown. Cool slightly. Remove from baking sheet and cool on wire rack. Frost cookies in petal pattern or around edges. Gently press "M&M's" Plain Chocolate Candies into frosting. Fill each flower pot with candies. Insert cookie flowers in candy-filled pots. Makes 18 flowerpots.

Fringed Ornament

Clear acetate sheet, medium weight
    (available at art supply stores in
    25" x 40" sheets)
Transparent tape
Scraps of clear plastic wrap

1/4 cup "M&M's" Plain or Peanut Chocolate
    Candies
White and red tissue paper
Scissors
Green crinkle ribbon

Cut a 3-1/2" x 4" acetate rectangle. Roll into a 3-1/2-inch long tube, overlapping edges 1/4 inch. Fasten with piece of tape along seam. Crush a scrap of plastic wrap, insert in one end of tube, close end of tube with piece of tape. Fill tube with candies. Close open end with scrap of plastic wrap and piece of tape as before. Cut two strips of white tissue paper, each 2-1/2" x 9-1/2". Fold each strip in half lengthwise. Cut into folded edge with scissors at 1/8-inch intervals, cutting 3/4 inch in from fold to make fringe. Wrap each cut strip around one end of candy-filled tube; tape in place. Repeat with red tissue. Tape red strips in place over white strips on tube. Fluff fringe with fingers. Cut 22-inch piece of green crinkle ribbon; tie each end to tube over red tissue. Makes 1 ornament.

Advent Candy Calendar

Hobby paint
1 (3/8" x 36") dowel
1-1/2 yds. (1/2-inch) red grosgrain ribbon
2 yds. each of 3/8-inch grosgrain ribbon
   in the following colors: purple, dark blue,
   red, light lavender, medium lavender,
   magenta
24 FUN SIZE Candies

24 (4-inch) squares blue cellophane
   (available at art supply stores)
Transparent tape
Artist's paintbrush
2 small screw eyes
Glossy paper in one or more colors
Black marker
Rubber cement

Paint dowel and let dry. Attach screw eyes to each end of dowel. Tie ends of 1/2-inch grosgrain ribbon to screw eyes in bows. Hang dowel horizontal by ribbon. Cut each length of 3/8-inch ribbon into three pieces of varying lengths with the shortest piece about 15 inches long. Tie each ribbon piece to dowel in a knot, so colors and lengths are mixed. Leave tails about 2 inches long. Wrap each FUN SIZE Candy in a cellophane square. Fasten with transparent tape. Tie a wrapped candy in end of each ribbon on dowel. Cut colored paper into stars, small trees, circles or other desired shapes. Mark a number 1 to 24, on each shape. Attach a number to each candy wrapper with rubber cement. Remove one piece each day, starting December 1. Makes 1 calendar.

Festive Easter Basket

Scissors
1 (11-1/4") circle white tagboard
1 (4-1/8" x 30") strip white tagboard
Stapler
Masking tape
1 (1" x 22") strip yellow tagboard
1 (1" x 22") strip orange tagboard
Yellow and orange crinkle ribbon,
   cut into 30" lengths
1 (36" length) plaid taffeta ribbon
Green cellophane grass
2 (1-lb.) bags FUN SIZE Candies—
   SNICKERS or MILKY WAY Bars

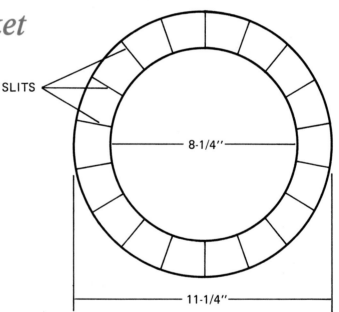

SLITS

8-1/4"

11-1/4"

With scissors, slit tagboard circle to make flaps as shown in drawing. Bend flaps along 8-1/4-inch circle to form basket bottom. Shape white tagboard strip into a cylinder with 8-1/4-inch diameter; staple closed. Place bottom of cylinder on circle; tape flaps to side of cylinder to make basket. Curve yellow and orange tagboard strips to form crisscrossed handle; insert ends into basket. Staple handle to inside of basket. Make pairs of vertical slits 1/2 inch apart around bottom of basket just above edge of flaps. Space pairs of slits 1-1/2 inches apart. Thread crinkle ribbon through a pair of slits and tie one piece of candy to basket. Curl ends of ribbon with scissors. Repeat around bottom of basket, then add row around top of basket. Tie several lengths of crinkle ribbon around handle; curl ribbon ends. Tie plaid ribbon in bow on top of handles. Fill basket with green cellophane grass. Makes 1 basket.

Candy Clown

1 (10" x 12") sheet of 1/4-inch Styrofoam
Blue, red and pink spray paint
Felt material:
    1/4 yd. blue
    1 (12-inch square) red
    1 (12-inch square) light pink
    Scraps of medium pink, lavender and black
White glue
6-1/2 yds. red (4-inch wide) florist's ribbon
Straight pins (optional)
1 (10-inch long) Styrofoam egg for body
1 roll of clear plastic wrap
4-1/3 (1-lb.) pkgs. "M&M's" Peanut
    Chocolate Candies or 2-1/2 (1-lb.) pkgs.
    "M&M's" Plain Chocolate Candies
About 75 twist ties from plastic storage bags
About 75 pipe cleaners
3 (1-inch) Styrofoam balls for buttons
Wooden picks
2 (2-inch long) Styrofoam eggs for nose
    and ears
1 (6-inch) Styrofoam ball for head
2 (2" x 4") pieces synthetic fur fabric
Blue thread and needle
2 (1/4" x 8") dowels with one end pointed
Florist's wire or other pliable, sturdy wire

Base:

Using the drawing on page 137 as a pattern, draw feet on Styrofoam sheet; cut out using kitchen knife. Spray paint feet blue and let dry. Cut red and blue shoe decorations from felt according to drawing. Glue decorations to feet as in photograph. Cut a 64-inch length of red ribbon. Glue or pin it to broad end of 10-inch Styrofoam egg, gathering it into a ruffle as you go. Glue broad end of egg to feet.

Body:

Tear 11-inch squares of plastic wrap off roll. Using two layers of plastic wrap, place 1/4 cup candies in center of square. Gather up corners, twist so candy is tightly encased. Fasten with a twist tie as close to candy as possible. Trim off excess plastic wrap with scissors, leaving a 1/2-inch tail. Wrap pipe cleaner around candy packet, keeping ends even. Fasten candy packet to body by inserting ends of pipe cleaner in egg. Begin at bottom of egg and work around in rows until the entire egg is covered. Place candy packets close to each other so Styrofoam does not show. Spray paint the 3 (1-inch) Styrofoam balls red. Dip end of wooden pick in white glue, insert in red ball. Dip other end of wooden pick in white glue, insert in front of body for button. Repeat with second red ball. Set aside third ball.

Head:

Cut one small Styrofoam egg in half lengthwise. Spray paint the two egg halves and the 6-inch Styrofoam ball pink. Use toothpicks and glue to fasten the 6-inch ball to top of large egg to make head. Cut a 26-inch length of red ribbon and gather around bottom of pink ball. Glue or pin into place. Make patterns for eyes, mouth, eyebrows and cheeks. Cut from felt according to colors listed in drawings. Glue to head as shown in photograph. Use toothpicks and glue to fasten a pink egg for nose and egg halves for ears. Glue fur pieces to head above each ear for hair. Cut 1/2 circle with a 6-inch radius from blue felt. Shape into cone and glue to close. Cut point from cone, glue remaining red Styrofoam ball to point. Glue hat on head in desired position.

Arms:

Make pattern for hand. Cut 4 hands from light pink felt. Glue 2 hands together around the edges. Glue other two together to make one pair. Leave center of hand open for dowel. Insert blunt end of each dowel into each hand. Fasten hand to dowel at wrist with wire. Cut twelve 12-inch lengths of red ribbon. Gather a strip of ribbon around the dowel. Fasten with wire 3/4 inch from ribbon edge. Push ruffle toward hand. Repeat making 6 ruffles on each dowel. Dip pointed end of dowel into glue. Insert in body as shown in photo.

Candy Clown Patterns

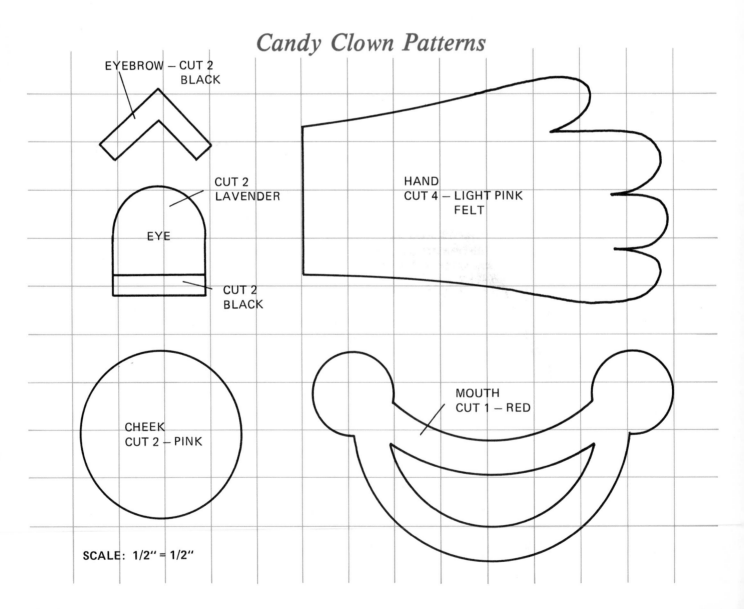

EYEBROW – CUT 2 BLACK

EYE — CUT 2 LAVENDER — CUT 2 BLACK

HAND CUT 4 – LIGHT PINK FELT

CHEEK CUT 2 – PINK

MOUTH CUT 1 – RED

SCALE: 1/2" = 1/2"

Candy Clown Pattern

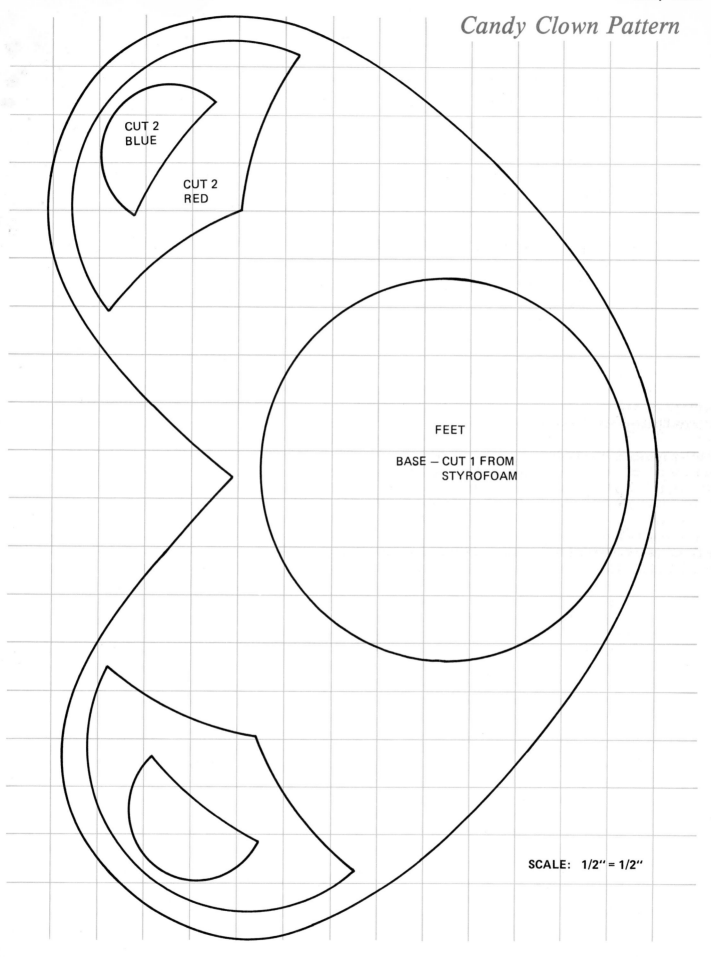

CUT 2
BLUE

CUT 2
RED

FEET

BASE — CUT 1 FROM
STYROFOAM

SCALE: 1/2″ = 1/2″

Candy Santa

Paper, ruler and pencil for pattern-making	4 (1-inch) Styrofoam balls
Small piece of cardboard	1 (4-inch) Styrofoam ball, for head
Small piece of aluminum foil	White glue
1 (1" x 20") black satin ribbon	3/4 yard shirred white eyelet trim
1 (6-1/2-inch) brandy snifter	1 (12-inch) square red felt
Straight pins	1 (12-inch) square white felt
Sheet of 1/2-inch Styrofoam	Rubber cement
Coping saw	1 (1-lb.) pkg. "M&M's" Plain or Peanut
Black, red and pink spray paint	Chocolate Candies

Make paper pattern for buckle, feet, arms, beard and mouth. Cut buckle from cardboard and cover with aluminum foil. Thread buckle onto black ribbon, wrap around center of snifter, fasten with straight pin or glue. Cut feet and arms from Styrofoam sheet using coping saw. Cut one of the small Styrofoam balls in half for cheeks. Cut 2 wedges from a second Styrofoam ball for eyes. Spray paint feet and eyes black, arms red. Paint the 4-inch Styrofoam ball, 1 small Styrofoam ball and cheeks pink. Cut beard and mouth from white and red felt. Fasten beard, eyes, nose and cheeks to head with straight pins and white glue if needed. Glue mouth over beard. Shape red felt into cone for hat, leaving a flap of felt. Glue to hold cone shape. Stitch eyelet trim to bottom edge of hat. Pin remaining small Styrofoam ball to end of cap. Pin or glue cap to head. Cut two 5-inch pieces of eyelet. Wrap around arms; fasten with straight pins. Attach feet to bottom of snifter and arms to sides of snifter as follows: Apply rubber cement to snifter and to Styrofoam. Let dry until tacky. Press Styrofoam against snifter. Fill snifter with "M&M's" Chocolate Candies. Place head on top of snifter. Repeat with remaining snifters. Makes 1 Santa.

Candy Santa Patterns

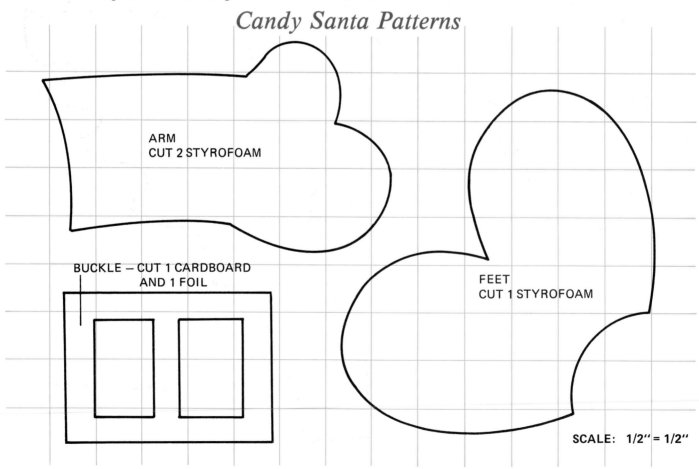

ARM
CUT 2 STYROFOAM

BUCKLE — CUT 1 CARDBOARD
AND 1 FOIL

FEET
CUT 1 STYROFOAM

SCALE: 1/2" = 1/2"

Candy Santa Patterns

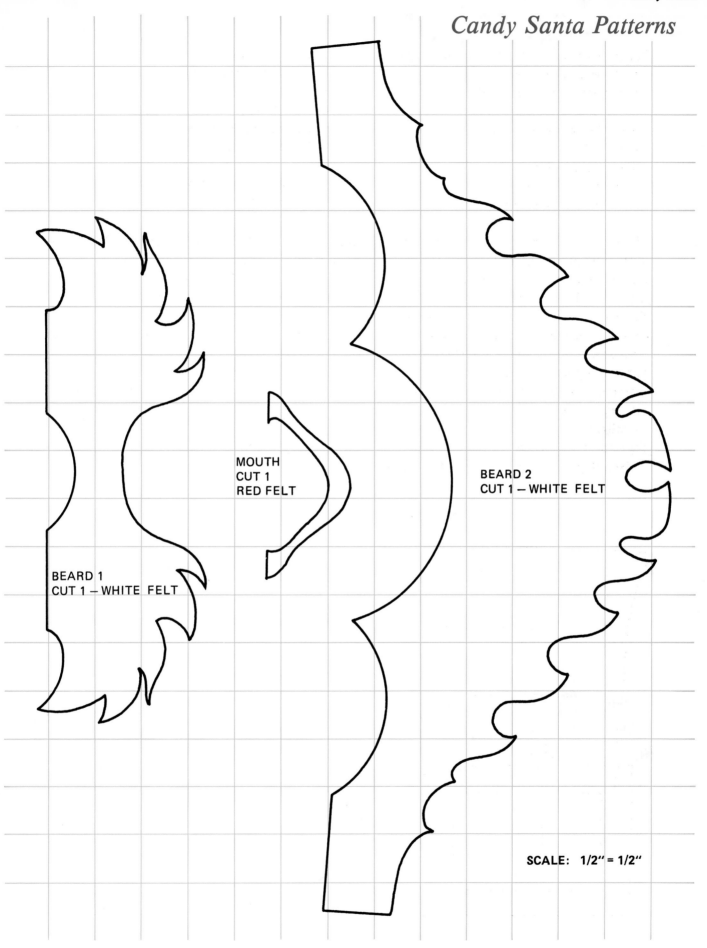

MOUTH
CUT 1
RED FELT

BEARD 1
CUT 1 — WHITE FELT

BEARD 2
CUT 1 — WHITE FELT

SCALE: 1/2" = 1/2"

Foil Party Cups

5 feet of aluminum foil
Scissors
Small saucer or dish
Small glass

Crinkle ribbon in desired shade
Cellophane tape
1 (1-lb.) pkg. "M&M's" Plain or Peanut
   Chocolate Candies

Tear off a 15-inch length of smooth aluminum foil. Fold in half with shiny side out. Using saucer as pattern, cut circles approximately 6 inches in diameter. Use each pair of circles as one piece. Place circle over inverted glass. Press foil to mold to shape of glass. Flare edges out. Fringe by cutting 3/4-inch slits around the edge. Tie crinkle ribbon around molded part. Fasten ribbon at sides with small piece of cellophane tape. Curl ribbon ends with scissors blade. Remove from glass. Fill cup with candies. Makes 4 cups.

Popcorn Clown

Scissors
Green, orange, yellow, red and black
   construction paper
1 (9-oz.) Styrofoam cup
Glue

Popcorn Ball about 4 inches in diameter,
   see page 124
Plastic wrap
1 (1-lb.) pkg. "M&M's" Plain Chocolate Candies
Thread

Cut a strip of green construction paper into 11" x 4-1/2" rectangle. Wrap around Styrofoam cup and glue to form a cylinder for the body of the clown. Cut a circle 6 inches in diameter from green paper. Cut out a 3-1/2" hole in the circle to form a ring. Cut 1-1/2" scallops along edge of ring. Cut through the ring at one point and overlap one scallop on each side of the cut; glue. Make six 1-inch cuts between 7 scallops opposite overlap making sure not to cut through the ring. Cut 18 orange circles 3/4 inch in diameter and 18 yellow circles 1/2 inch in diameter. Glue yellow circles to center of orange circles. Glue 5 of these circles to the slit scallops. Place green scalloped ring on cylinder formed with Styrofoam cup. Wrap popcorn ball in plastic wrap. Gather and tie ends. Place on Styrofoam cup with plastic wrap ends in cup. Cut a 6-inch circle from green construction paper. Slit to middle and overlap to form cone-shaped hat that will rest on popcorn ball; glue. Wrap 10 "M&M's" Plain Chocolate Candies in plastic wrap. Tie with thread. Make 12 candy clusters. Staple ends of plastic wrap to inside bottom edge of hat. Cut orange paper fringe hair; glue to inside of hat. Hair should hang under candy clusters. Glue a row of orange and yellow circles on outside bottom edge of hat. Cut four 1-inch orange circles and fringe edges. Cut four 1/2-inch yellow circles and glue to center of fringed orange circles. Glue one fringed circle to top of hat. Glue remaining circles to green cylinder base for buttons. Cut eyes, nose and mouth from colored paper; glue to plastic wrapped popcorn ball. Makes 1 clown.

Ding Bat Bird

Paper
Ruler
Pencil
1 (12"x 14") sheet of 1/4-inch Styrofoam
Pink, yellow and green spray paint
1 (4-inch) Styrofoam ball, head
1 (1" x 3/4") Styrofoam cylinder, neck
1 (6-inch long) Styrofoam egg, body
Large straight pins, optional
White glue
1-1/2 (1-lb.) pkgs. "M&M's" Peanut Chocolate
    Candies or 1 (1-lb.) pkg. "M&M's" Plain
    Chocolate Candies
1 roll clear plastic wrap
About 65 twist ties (from plastic storage bags)
About 65 pipe cleaners
Wooden picks
2 plastic eyes
Scraps of red felt
Cluster of maribou or other feathers
20-inch length of green ribbon, 1/2-inch wide

Body:

Make paper pattern for feet, wings, tail, beak and bow according to drawings on pages 142 and 143. Use a kitchen knife to cut these pieces from Styrofoam sheet. Spray paint pieces according to colors listed on drawings. Wings, tail and bow are striped. While painted wings and tail are wet and pliable, bend narrow ends at a 45-degree to 60-degree angle. Spray paint Styrofoam ball and cylinder pink. Let dry. Fasten broad end of Styrofoam egg to center of feet with straight pins or glue or both. Cover egg with candy as follows: Tear 11-inch squares of plastic wrap off roll. Using 2 layers of plastic wrap, place 1/4 cup "M&M's" Chocolate Candies in center of square. Gather up corners, twist so candy is tightly enclosed. Fasten with a twist tie as close to candy as possible. Trim off excess plastic wrap with scissors, leaving a 1/2-inch tail. Wrap pipe cleaner around candy packet, keeping ends even. Fasten candy packet to body by inserting ends of pipe cleaner into egg. Begin at bottom of egg and work around in rows until entire egg is covered. Place candy packets close together so Styrofoam does not show. Insert wooden pick dipped in glue in bent end of wing. Fasten wing to egg at side by inserting wooden pick. Repeat with other wing on other side. Fasten tail to back of egg in same way.

Head:

Glue pink cylinder to pink ball (head) for neck. Glue bow to top of head. Glue feathers to top of bow. Insert 2 to 3 wooden picks dipped in glue into end of neck cylinder. Dip remaining ends in glue and insert in top of body. Tie green ribbon in bow around neck. Glue eyes in front of head. Cut red felt tongue according to drawing on page 143. Sandwich felt tongue between beak. Glue in place at broad end only. Fasten beak and tongue to head under eyes by dipping toothpicks in glue and inserting in broad end of beak and then to head. Pull beak apart slightly to allow the tongue to show.

BOW TIE – CUT 1
STYROFOAM

GREEN

BIRD FEET
BASE
CUT 1 STYROFOAM
SPRAY PAINT GREEN

YELLOW

PINK

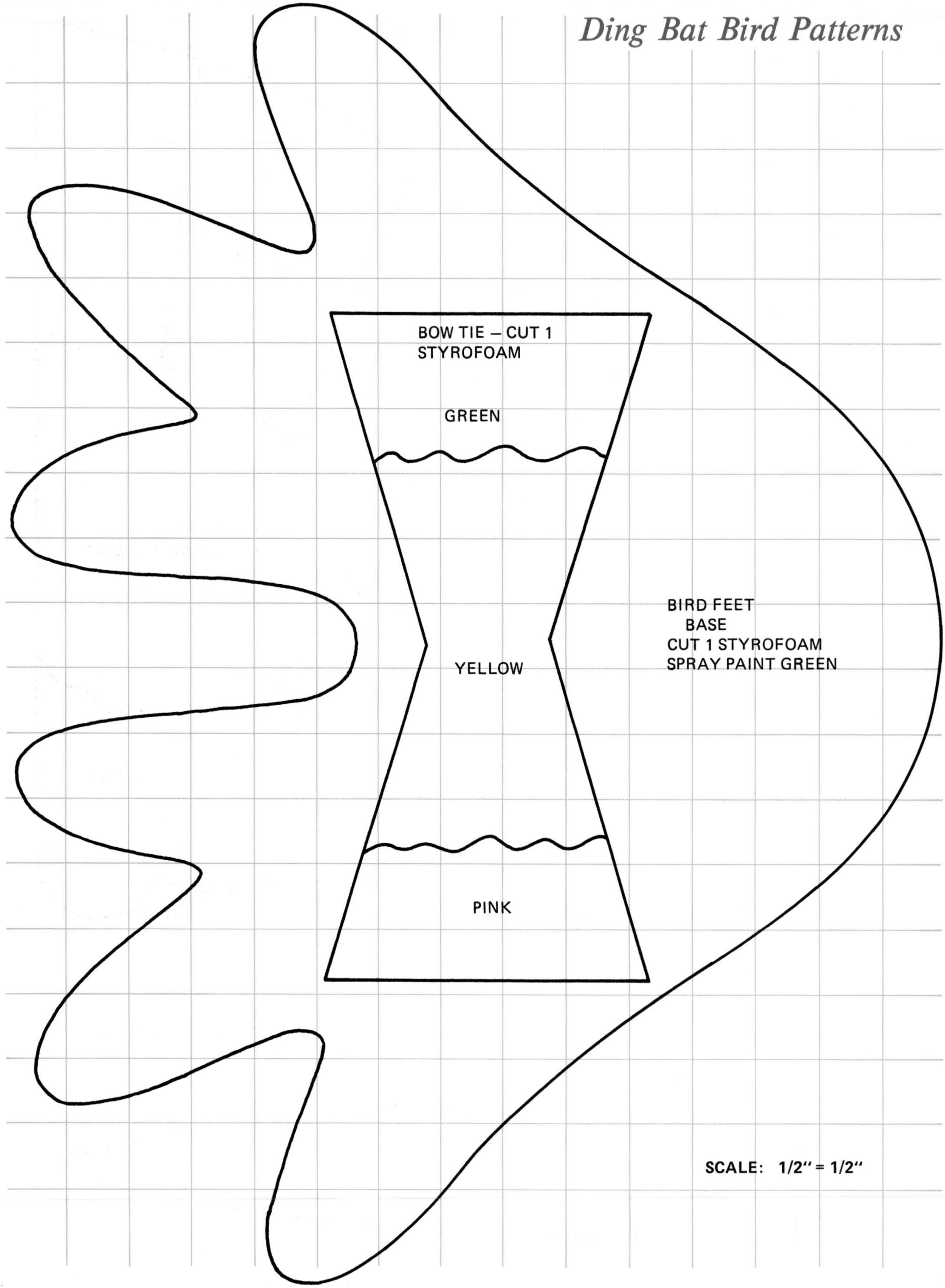

SCALE: 1/2″ = 1/2″

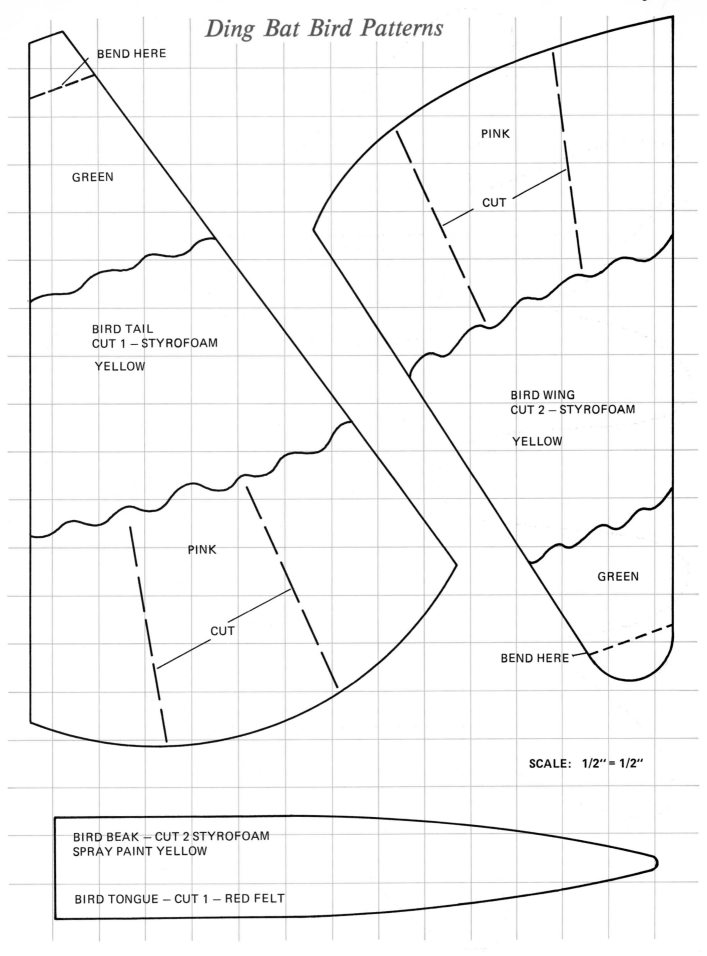

Ding Bat Bird Patterns

BEND HERE

GREEN

BIRD TAIL
CUT 1 – STYROFOAM

YELLOW

PINK

CUT

PINK

CUT

PINK

CUT

BIRD WING
CUT 2 – STYROFOAM

YELLOW

GREEN

BEND HERE

SCALE: 1/2″ = 1/2″

BIRD BEAK – CUT 2 STYROFOAM
SPRAY PAINT YELLOW

BIRD TONGUE – CUT 1 – RED FELT

Leaping Frog

Paper
Ruler
Pencil
1 (12" x 14") sheet of 1/4-inch Styrofoam
1 (4-inch) Styrofoam ball, head
2 (1-1/2-inch) Styrofoam balls, eyes
Green spray paint
1 (6-inch long) Styrofoam egg, body
Large straight pins (optional)
White glue
5-1/2 (1-lb.) pkgs. "M&M's" Peanut Chocolate
    Candies or 7 (1-lb.) pkgs. "M&M's" Plain
    Chocolate Candies
1 roll clear plastic wrap
About 50 twist ties (from plastic storage bags)
About 50 pipe cleaners
Wooden picks
Scraps of light pink, white and red felt
Two adhesive-backed eyes
4-inch satin bow
Decorative bumble bee

Body:
Make paper pattern for feet and hands according to drawings. Use a kitchen knife to cut feet and 2 hands from Styrofoam sheet. Spray feet, hands and Styrofoam balls green. While painted hands are still wet and pliable, bend narrow ends at 45-degree to 60-degree angle. Let dry. Fasten broad end of Styrofoam egg to center of feet with straight pins, glue or both. Remove all green "M&M's" Plain Chocolate Candies from packages for use on frog. Cover egg with candy as follows: Tear 11-inch squares of clear plastic wrap off roll. Using 2 layers of plastic wrap, place 1/4 cup green candies in center of square. Gather up corners and twist so candy is tightly encased. Fasten with a twist tie as close to candy as possible. Trim off excess plastic wrap with scissors, leaving a 1/2-inch tail. Wrap pipe cleaner around end of candy packet, keeping ends even. Fasten candy packet to body by inserting ends of pipe cleaner into egg. Begin at bottom of egg and work around in rows until entire egg is covered. Place candy packets close together so Styrofoam does not show.

Head:
Using a kitchen knife, cut a wedge from large green Styrofoam ball. Remove about 1/5 of ball to make mouth. Cut a slice off each small green Styrofoam ball to make eyes. Cut 2 semi-circular pieces of light pink felt to fit mouth; glue in place. Cut 2 white felt circles to fit over flat portion of eyes; glue in place. Press adhesive-backed eyes in center of white felt. Glue bow to back of head. Cut an oval tongue 5/8" x 5" from red felt. Taper at one end. Glue bumblebee to broad end of tongue. Glue narrow end of tongue to center of mouth. Fasten head to body with wooden picks and glue.

Leaping Frog Pattern

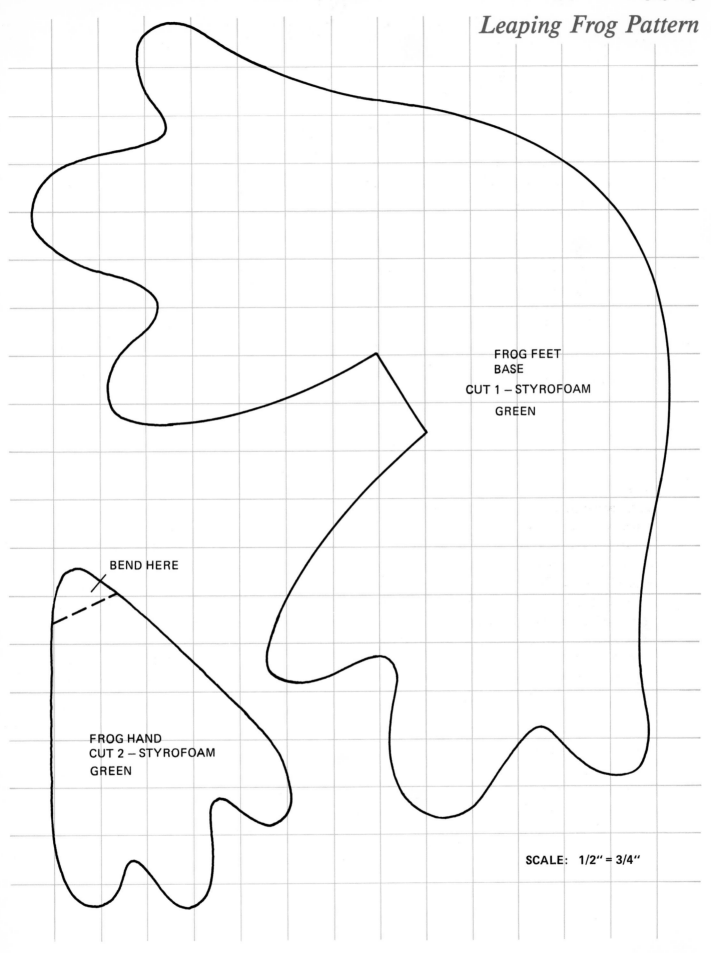

FROG FEET
BASE

CUT 1 – STYROFOAM

GREEN

BEND HERE

FROG HAND
CUT 2 – STYROFOAM

GREEN

SCALE: 1/2" = 3/4"

Peanut Peggy Doll

Paper
Ruler
Pencil
Felt material:
    2 12-inch squares, light pink
    1 12-inch square, white
    1 12-inch square, red
    Scraps of lavender, medium pink and black
2 pieces lace (1/2" x 1-3/4")
2 small white buttons
Green woven florists ribbon (4" x 90")
1 (10-inch) long Styrofoam egg for body
Straight pins, optional
White glue
4-1/3 (1-lb.) pkgs. "M&M's" Peanut Chocolate
    Candies or 2-1/2 (1-lb.) pkgs. "M&M's"
    Plain Chocolate Candies
1 roll clear plastic wrap
About 75 twist ties from plastic storage bags
About 75 pipe cleaners, 2 inches long
Pink spray paint
1 (6-inch) Styrofoam ball, for head
1(1/2-inch) Styrofoam ball, for nose
Wooden picks
62 yards yellow 3-ply synthetic yarn

Legs and Body:
Make paper pattern for legs, socks, shoes and arms according to drawings on page 148. Cut legs and arms from pink felt, socks from white felt and shoes from red felt as indicated in drawings. Glue socks and shoes onto legs. Glue lace in place at top of socks and buttons in place on each shoe. Set arms aside. Gather a 60-inch length of green ribbon around broad end of Styrofoam egg; attach to egg with straight pins, glue or both. Glue legs to bottom of egg as shown in photograph. Cover Styrofoam egg with candy as follows: Tear 11-inch squares of plastic wrap off roll. Using 2 layers of plastic wrap, place 1/4 cup of "M&M's" Chocolate Candies in center of square. Gather up corners, twist so candy is tightly encased. Fasten with a twist tie as close to candy as possible. Trim off excess plastic wrap with scissors, leaving a 1/2-inch tail. Wrap pipe cleaner around end of candy packet, keeping ends even. Attach candy packet to body by inserting ends of pipe cleaner into egg. Begin at bottom of egg and work around in rows until entire egg is covered. Place candy packets close to each other so Styrofoam does not show.

Head:

Spray paint large (head) and small (nose) Styrofoam balls pink and let dry. Make paper patterns for eyes, mouth and cheeks according to drawings below. Cut from felt. Glue eyes, mouth and cheeks to large Styrofoam ball as shown in photograph. Use wooden pick and glue to fasten small ball to face as nose. Gather a 30-inch length of green ribbon around bottom of head; fasten to head with straight pins or glue. For hair, cut 100 pieces of yarn, each 22 inches long. Gather into a bunch with ends even. Cut a 12-inch length of yarn, tie around center of bunch in 8-inch loop as shown in drawing. Loop around yarn will be loose. Carefully place on top of head with loop running from front to back. Pin and glue in place along loop, evenly distributing "hair" along loop so hair covers back, sides and front of head. Trim front hairs for bangs. Tie cotton ribbon into bow; pin and glue to top of head. Use wooden picks and glue to fasten head to body. Pin arms to body under ribbon ruffle at neck.

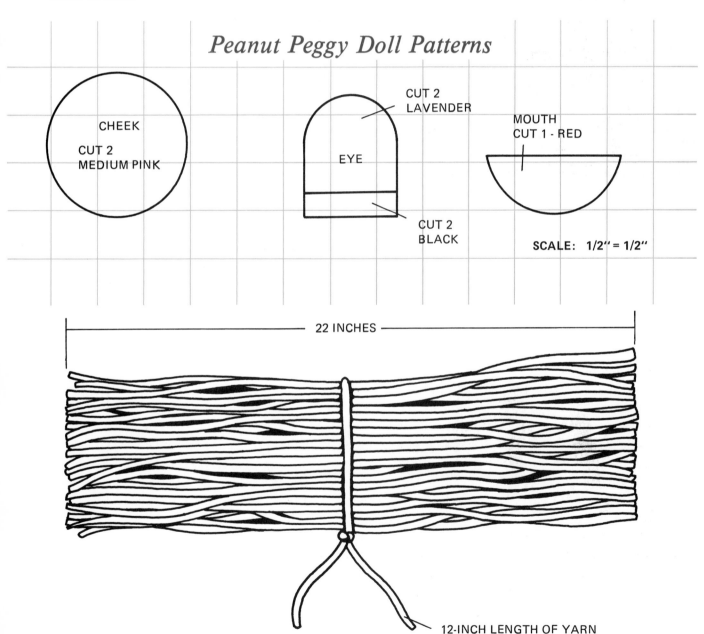

Peanut Peggy Doll Patterns

CHEEK

CUT 2
MEDIUM PINK

CUT 2
LAVENDER

EYE

CUT 2
BLACK

MOUTH
CUT 1 - RED

SCALE: 1/2" = 1/2"

22 INCHES

12-INCH LENGTH OF YARN

Peanut Peggy Doll Patterns

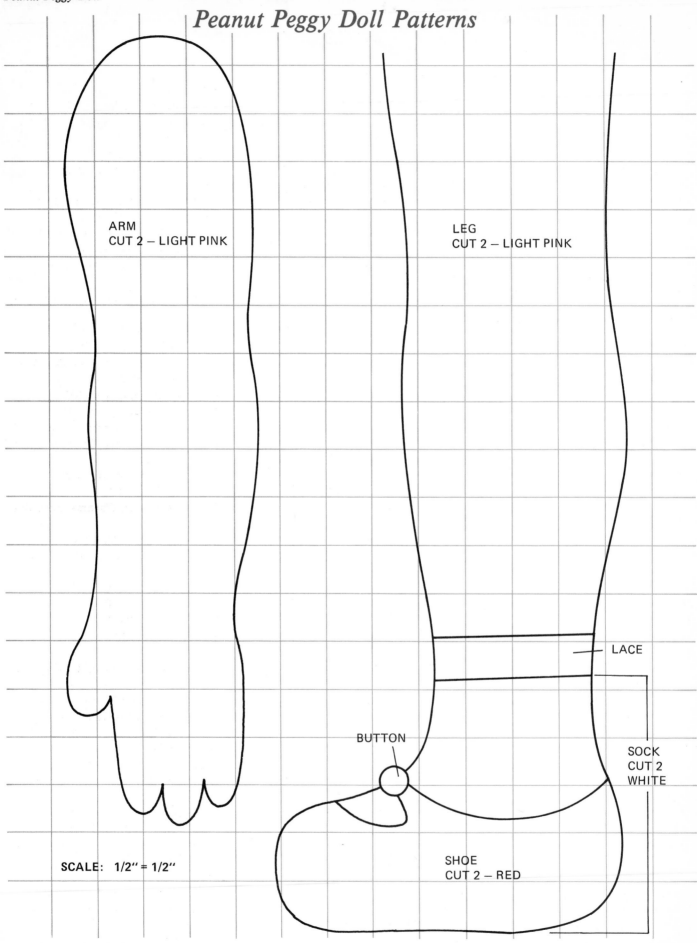

ARM
CUT 2 — LIGHT PINK

LEG
CUT 2 — LIGHT PINK

LACE

BUTTON

SOCK
CUT 2
WHITE

SHOE
CUT 2 — RED

SCALE: 1/2″ = 1/2″

Index

A

Advent Candy Calendar 134
Alaskas, Baked Chocolate 8
Almond Chocolate Ice Cream 79
Almond Sauce, Chocolate 102
Almond Twists, Holiday 114
Angel-Food Cake, Peanutty 59
Angel Pie, Orange Chocolate 62
Angelic Dessert 83
Apple Tart, Peanut-Caramel 11
Apple Turnovers, Super Easy 10
Aspic, Tomato 96

B

Baked Chocolate Alaskas 8
Baked Squash With Crunch Topping 95
Balloon Cake 34
Ball Tree Ornament 132
Balls, Chocolate 115
Banana Bars 14
Banana Cream Pie, Caramel 16
Banana Chocolate Floats 14
Banana Split Crepes 69
Bananas Praline 73
Bars
    Banana Bars 14
    Confetti Bars 87
    Party Perfect Bars 12
    Peanut Meringue Bars 31
    Pirate's Delight 87
    Rainbow Oat Bars 85
Bavarian Easter Egg 54
Bavarian, Sweet Cherry 78
Beef Stew, Hungarian 95
Beets, Tart Sweet 98
Beverages
    Calypso Chocolate 21
    Hot Maple Chocolate 73
    Ice Cream Nog 23
    Easy Hot Chocolate 108
    Mocha Brûlot 116
    Hot Russian Punch 119
Bird, Ding Bat 141-143
Black Bottom Pie 70
Bread Pudding, Today's 9
Breads
    Bunny & Duck Easter Breads 47
    Choco-Banana Muffins 48
    Christmas Tree Bread 124
    Easter Flower Pot Breads 58
    Easter Fruit Bread 50
    Fluted Orange Bread 52
    Hot Caramel Pecan Rolls 19
    Hot Cross Buns 56
    Lucia Buns 122
    Peanutty Date Bread 87
    Sticky Buns 24
    Treasure Puffs 86
Brownie Sundae 108
Brownies, Caramel-Chocolate 112
Brûlée, Peanut Topped Creme 75
Brûlot, Mocha 116
Bunny & Duck Easter Breads 47
Buns, Hot Cross 56
Buns, Lucia 122
Buns, Sticky 24
Butterfly Cake 41
Buttery Flower Cookies 18

C

Cakes (also see Take A Cake And Make It
    Great)
    Angelic Dessert 83
    Chocolate Fruit Cake 119
    Chocolate Torte 66
    Easter Bunny Cake 52
    Holiday Cake Roll 117
    Mandarin Orange Roll 64
    Peach-Glazed Spice Cake 68
    Peanutty Angel-Food Cake 59
    Valentine Cake 30
Calico Meringues 111
Calypso Chocolate 21
Candy Christmas Heart 131
Candy Clown 135-137
Candy Cone Ornament 130
Candy Pudding Cake 71
Candy Santa 138-139
Caramel-Banana Cream Pie 16
Caramel-Chocolate Brownies 112
Caramel-Orange Cookie Slices 89
Caramel Soufflé, Favorite 84
Caramel Squares, Peanutty 92
Centerpiece, Poppy 128
Cereal Square Snacks 108
Charlotte, Elegant Coffee 80
Cheese Egg, Chocolate 48
Cheesecake, Chocolate Crunch 77
Cheesecake Cups, Chocolate 26
Cheesecake, Tangy Topped 48
Cheesey Crepes In Fruit Sauce 73
Cherry Bavarian, Sweet 78
Cherry Pie, Chocolate 15
Chicken Mole, Hacienda 97
Chicken Salad, Gado Gado 95
Chicken With Peanut Sauce, Polynesian 98
Chilled Mocha Soufflé 60
Chinese Checker Cake 39
Choco-Banana Muffins 48
Chocolate-Almond Sauce 102
Chocolate & Ice Cream Tarts 107
Chocolate Balls 115
Chocolate Cheese Egg 48
Chocolate Cheesecake Cups 26
Chocolate Cherry Pie 15
Chocolate Crunch Cheesecake 77
Chocolate Dessert Crepes 63
Chocolate Drop Cookies 112
Chocolate Frosting, Orange 101
Chocolate Fruit Cake 119
Chocolate Gems 122
Chocolate Mousse, Meringue Hearts With
    30
Chocolate Nests 51
Chocolate Orange Ribbon Cake 40
Chocolate & Peanut Popcorn Balls 119
Chocolate Pound Cake 40
Chocolate Sauce, Creamy 102
Chocolate Sauce, Mystery 104
Chocolate-Streusel Topped Coffeecake 25
Chocolate: The World's Favorite Flavor 3
Chocolate Torte 66
Chocolate Torte, Strawberry 38
Chocolate Waffles 69
Christmas, see Fun Christmas Food And
    Decorations
Christmas Cookies, Ginger 120
Christmas Heart, Candy 131
Christmas Tree Bread 124
Christmas Tree, Flocked 132
Circle Pop Cookies 106
Clown, Candy 135-137
Clown, Popcorn 140
Cobcakes 89
Cocktail Meatballs, Sweet & Tangy 100
Coconut Cream Pie 56
Coconut Ice Cream Pie 84
Coconut Topped Chocolate Cake 36
Coeur à la Crème, Special 28
Coffee Charlotte, Elegant 80
Coffeecakes
    Chocolate-Streusel Topped Coffeecake
    25
    Holiday Almond Twists 114
    Orange Marmalade Coffeecake 116
    Peanut-Apricot Coffeecake 114
Cones, Confetti Cream 9
Confetti Bars 87
Confetti Cream Cones 9
Consumer Assurance of Quality 5
Conversation Pieces 94-100
Cookie Planters, Spring Flower 133

Index

Cookie-Topped Cupcakes 50
Cookies (also see Bars and Squares)
   Buttery Flower Cookies 18
   Caramel-Orange Cookie Slices 89
   Chocolate Balls 115
   Chocolate Drop Cookies 112
   Circle Pop Cookies 106
   Dogwood Blossoms 54
   Double-Decker Heart Cookies 28
   Easter Cookie Baskets 45
   Easter Cookie Fantasies 55
   Fun Center Log Slices 110
   Ginger Christmas Cookies 120
   Hidden Treasure Cookies 93
   No-Bake Peanut Drop Cookies 110
   Oatmeal Cookies 19
   Owl Cookies 90-91
   Peanutty Peanut Butter Cookies 116
   Polka Dot Specials 92
   Santa's Favorite Cookies 120
   Sitting Pretties 53
   Snowball Cookies 112
   Strawberry Cookie Tortes 29
   Super Trio Cookies 12
   Surprise-Filled Cookie Squares 107
   Wonder Cookies 105
Cooking Tips 7
Cottage Cake 42-43
Crafts, see Creative Crafts
Cream Puff Crown 66-67
Creamy Chocolate Sauce 102
Creative Crafts 127-148
Crème Brûlée, Peanut Topped 75
Crepes
   Banana Split Crepes 69
   Cheesey Crepes In Fruit Sauce 73
   Chocolate Dessert Crepes 63
   Delicious Filled Crepes 60
   Ice Cream Crepes With Almond Sauce 20
   Marmalade Crepes 63
Croquettes With Tangy Sauce, Turkey 97
Crown, Cream Puff 66-67
Crumb Cupcakes 11
Crunchy Peanut Cake 36
Cupcakes
   Chocolate Cheesecake Cups 26
   Cobcakes 89
   Cookie-Topped Cupcakes 50
   Crumb Cupcakes 11
Cups, Foil Party 140

D

Date Bread, Peanutty 87
Delicious Filled Crepes 60

Dessert Crepes, Chocolate 63
Dessert Sauce, Magic 104
Ding Bat Bird 141-143
Do Ahead—Take From Freezer Or
   Refrigerator 76-84
Dogwood Blossoms 54
Doll, Peanut Peggy 146-148
Double-Decker Heart Cookies 28
Drop Cookies, Chocolate 112
Drop Cookies, No-Bake Peanut 110

E

Easter 45-58
Easter Basket Cake 46
Easter Bunny Cake 52
Easter Cookie Baskets 45
Easter Cookie Fantasies 55
Easter Egg, Bavarian 54
Easter Flower Pot Breads 58
Easter Fruit Bread 50
Easy Hot Chocolate 108
Easy Pear Kuchen 55
Egg, Chocolate Cheese 48
Elegant Coffee Charlotte 80
Elegant Desserts 59-67

F

Favorite Caramel Soufflé 84
Festive Easter Basket 134
Festive Frosted Loaf Cake 42
Flan, Orangy Peach Caramel 64
Floats, Banana Chocolate 14
Flocked Christmas Tree 132
Flower Pot Breads, Easter 58
Fluted Orange Bread 52
Foil Party Cups 140
Fondue, Something Special 21
For Kids 105-112
Fortress Cake 33
FOREVER YOURS Bars 4, 15, 62, 67, 95,
   97, 107, 112
Fringed Ornament 133
Frog, Leaping 144-145
Frostings, see Top It Off
Frozen Choco-Almond Mousse 79
Frozen Peach Yogurt Pie 82
Fruit Cake, Chocolate 119
Fun Center Log Slices 110
Fun Christmas Food And Decorations
   113-126
FUN SIZE MARATHON Candies 10, 33,
   129, 131
FUN SIZE MILKY WAY Candies 8, 60,
   108, 129, 131, 134

FUN SIZE 3 MUSKETEERS Candies 8,
   33, 60, 108, 129, 131
FUN SIZE SNICKERS Candies 8, 60,
   108, 129, 131, 134

G

Gado Gado Chicken Salad 95
Ginger Christmas Cookies 120
"Gorp" Power Pack Snack 110
Guarantee of Satisfaction 5

H

Hacienda Chicken Mole 97
Ham And Chutney Peaches,
   Tangy Glazed 94
Heart, Candy Christmas 131
Heart Cookies, Double Decker 28
Hearts With Chocolate Mousse, Meringue
   30-31
Hidden Treasure Cookies 93
History of chocolate 3
Holiday Almond Twists 114
Holiday Cake Roll 117
Hot Caramel Pecan Rolls 19
Hot Chocolate, Easy 108
Hot Cross Buns 56
Hot Maple Chocolate 73
Hot Russian Punch 119
Hungarian Beef Stew 95

I

Ice Cream
   Noël Tortoni 125
   Almond Chocolate Ice Cream 79
Ice Cream Crepes With Almond Sauce 20
Ice Cream Nog 23
Ice Cream Pie, Coconut 84
Ice Cream Pie, Neapolitan 74
Ice Cream Pie, Pumpkin 16
Ingredients Make The Difference 6-7
Instant Desserts For Unexpected Guests
   68-75
Italian Pastry Shells 126

J

Jack-O-Lantern Piñata 129

K

Kuchen, Easy Pear 55

L

Ladybug Cakes 32
Lamb Patties With Fruit Sauce 100
Leaping Frog 144-145

Little Celebrations 8-19
Loaf Cake, Festive Frosted 42
Log Slices, Fun Center 110
Lucia Buns 122

M
"M&M's" Peanut Chocolate Candies 4, 9, 24, 33, 34, 39, 41, 42, 45, 46, 47, 50, 51 52, 53, 74, 77, 87, 93, 105, 107, 110, 114, 116, 119, 120, 124, 129, 132, 133, 135, 138, 140, 141, 144, 146
"M&M's" Plain Chocolate Candies 4, 12, 14, 18, 21, 23, 24, 25, 30, 32, 33, 34, 35, 38, 39, 40, 41, 42, 45, 47, 48, 50, 51, 52, 54, 55, 56, 58, 62, 63, 66, 69, 70, 73, 74, 76, 77, 80, 84, 89, 90, 92, 101, 102, 103, 104, 105, 106, 108, 110, 111, 112, 114, 116, 117, 119, 120, 122, 125, 126, 127, 128, 129, 132, 133, 135, 138, 140, 141, 144, 146
Macaroon Nougats 21
Magic Dessert Sauce 104
Mahogany Pie 84
Main Dishes, see Conversation Pieces
Mandarin Orange Roll 64
MARATHON Bars 5, 11, 14, 16, 19, 41, 64, 69, 89, 119
Marmalade Crepes 63
MARS Almond Bars 4, 14, 66, 77, 79, 102, 107, 113, 129, 130
Marshmallow Dessert, Peanut 69
Marshmallow Sauce, Rich 103
Meatballs, Sweet & Tangy Cocktail 100
Meringues, Calico 111
Meringue Hearts With Chocolate Mousse 30-31
Meringue Pears 18
Meringue, Valentine 26
Mexican Sunrise Salad 98
MILKY WAY Bars 4, 21, 26, 28, 29, 33, 36, 48, 60, 62, 67, 80, 83, 84, 95, 97, 106, 108, 112, 121, 129, 130
Milky Wonder Cake 33
Mocha Brûlot 116
Mocha Mousse 76
Mocha Nut Mousse In Patty Shells 71
Mocha Pots de Crème 63
Mocha Puff Pyramid 113
Mocha Soufflé, Chilled 60
Molded Rice Pudding 61
Mole, Hacienda Chicken 97
Mousse, Frozen Choco-Almond 79
Mousse In Patty Shells, Mocha Nut 71
Mousse, Mocha 76

Mousse With Poached Peaches, Praline 82-83
MUNCH Peanut Bars 5, 11, 16, 19, 23, 31, 33, 36, 56, 59, 64, 69, 73, 75, 82, 87, 90, 94, 95, 97, 98, 116, 129
Mystery Chocolate Sauce 104

N
Napoleons In-A-Hurry 67
Neapolitan Ice Cream Pie 74
Nests, Chocolate 51
No-Bake Peanut Drop Cookies 110
Noel Tortoni 125
No-Trick Halloween Treats 85-93
Nougats, Macaroon 21
Nutty Sweet Potato Pie 74

O
Oat & Nut Squares 14
Oat Bars, Rainbow 85
Oatmeal Cookies 19
Orange Blosson Cake 35
Orange Blossom Trifle 80
Orange Bread, Fluted 52
Orange-Chocolate Angel Pie 62
Orange-Chocolate Frosting 101
Orange Cookie Slices, Caramel 89
Orange Marmalade Coffeecake 116
Orange Roll, Mandarin 64
Orangy Peach Caramel Flan 64
Ornaments
  Ball Tree Ornament 132
  Candy Christmas Heart 131
  Candy Cone Ornament 130
  Fringed Ornament 133
Owl Cookies 90-91

P
Parfaits With Chocolate Sauce, Strawberry 24
Party Perfect Bars 12
Pastry Shells, Italian 126
Patties With Fruit Sauce, Lamb 100
Peach Caramel Flan, Orangy 64
Peach-Glazed Spice Cake 68
Peach Yogurt Pie, Frozen 82
Peanut-Apricot Coffeecake 114
Peanut Butter Cookies, Peanutty 116
Peanut Cake, Crunchy 36
Peanut-Caramel Apple Tart 11
Peanut Crumb Pumpkin Pie 90
Peanut Marshmallow Dessert 69
Peanut Meringue Bars 31
Peanut Peggy Doll 146-148

Peanut Squares 107
Peanut Topped Crème Brûlée 75
Peanutty Angel-Food Cake 59
Peanutty Caramel Squares 92
Peanutty Date Bread 87
Peanutty Peanut Butter Cookies 116
Pear Kuchen, Easy 55
Pear Sundae, Zesty 71
Pears, Meringue 18
Pears Hélène 62
Pecan Rolls, Hot Caramel 19
Pies
  Black Bottom Pie 70
  Caramel-Banana Cream Pie 16
  Chocolate Cherry Pie 15
  Coconut Cream Pie 56
  Coconut Ice Cream Pie 84
  Frozen Peach Yogurt Pie 82
  Mahogany Pie 84
  Neapolitan Ice Cream Pie 74
  Nutty Sweet Potato Pie 74
  Orange-Chocolate Angel Pie 62
  Peanut Crumb Pumpkin Pie 90
  Pumpkin Ice Cream Pie 16
  Velvet Pie Supreme 79
Piñata, Jack-O-Lantern 129
Pineapple Upside-Down Cake 35
Pirate's Delight 87
Polka Dot Specials 92
Polynesian Chicken With Peanut Sauce 98
Popcorn Balls, Chocolate & Peanut 119
Popcorn Balls, Zesty 124
Popcorn Chain 127
Popcorn Clown 140
Poppy Centerpiece 128
Pots de Crème, Mocha 63
Pound Cake, Chocolate 40
Powdered Sugar Icing 102
Praline, Bananas 73
Praline Mousse With Poached Peaches 82-83
Pudding Cake, Candy 71
Pudding, Molded Rice 61
Pudding, Today's Bread 9
Pumpkin Ice Cream Pie 16
Pumpkin Pie, Peanut Crumb 90
Pyramid, Mocha Puff 113

R
Rainbow Oat Bars 85
Ribbon Cake, Chocolate Orange 40
Rice Pudding, Molded 61
Rich Marshmallow Sauce 103
Rolls, Hot Caramel Pecan 19

Index

Rum Chocolate Tarts 77
Russian Punch, Hot 119

S

Salad, Mexican Sunrise 98
Santa, Candy 138-139
Santa's Favorite Cookies 120
Sauces, see Top It Off
Shortcake, Strawberry Crunch 23
Sitting Pretties, 53
Snack, "Gorp" Power Pack 110
SNICKERS Bars 5, 24, 26, 28, 35, 36, 40, 61, 64, 68, 71, 74, 84, 92, 106, 108, 110, 112, 129, 130
Snowball Cookies 112
Something Special Fondue 21
Soufflé, Chilled Mocha 60
Soufflé, Favorite Caramel 84
Special Coeur à la Crème 28
Spice Cake, Peach-Glazed 68
Spicy Steamed Pudding 121
Spring Flower Cookie Planters 133
Squares
    Caramel Chocolate Brownies 112
    Cereal Square Snacks 108
    Chocolate Gems 122
    Oat & Nut Squares 14
    Peanut Squares 107
    Peanutty Caramel Squares 92
    Surprise-Filled Cookie Squares 107
Squash With Crunch Topping, Baked 95

STARBURST Fruit Chews 5, 41, 48, 71, 73, 85, 94, 96, 98, 100, 104, 119, 124, 129, 130
Steamed Pudding, Spicy 121
Sticky Buns 24
Storing Your Candy 7
Strawberry Chocolate Torte 38
Strawberry Cookie Tortes 29
Strawberry Crunch Shortcake 23
Strawberry Parfaits With Chocolate Sauce 24
Sundae, Brownie 108
Sundae, Zesty Pear 71
Super-Easy Apple Turnovers 10
Super Trio Cookies 12
Surprise-Filled Cookie Squares 107
Sweet & Tangy Cocktail Meatballs 100
Sweet Cherry Bavarian 78
Sweet Potato Pie, Nutty 74

T

Take A Cake And Make It Great 32-45
Tangy Glazed Ham And Chutney Peaches 94
Tangy Topped Cheesecake 48
Tart, Peanut-Caramel Apple 11
Tart Sweet Beets 98
Tarts, Chocolate & Ice Cream 107
Tarts, Rum Chocolate 77
The Choice Is Yours 4
3 MUSKETEERS Bars 4, 11, 21, 30, 33, 38 44, 55, 63, 71, 78, 79, 86, 102, 115, 129, 130

Today's Bread Pudding 9
Tomato Aspic 96
Top It Off 101-104
Torte, Chocolate 66
Torte, Strawberry Chocolate 38
Tortes, Strawberry Cookie 29
Tortoni, Noël 125
Treasure Puffs 86
Trifle, Orange Blossom 80
Trio Cookies, Super 12
Triple-Decker Cake 44
Turkey Croquettes With Tangy Sauce 97
Turnovers, Super Easy Apple 10
Twists, Holiday Almond 114

V

Valentine Cake 30
Valentine Delights 20-31
Valentine Meringue 26
Vegetables, see Conversation Pieces
Velvet Pie Supreme 79

W

Waffles, Chocolate 69
Why Cook With M&M/MARS Products 3
Wonder Cookies 105

Z

Zesty Pear Sundae 71
Zesty Popcorn Balls 124

CONVERSION TO METRIC MEASURE				
ENGLISH		**METRIC**	**FAHRENHEIT (F)**	**CELSIUS (C)**
1/4 teaspoon	=	1.25 milliliters	175°	80°
1/2 teaspoon	=	2.5 milliliters	200°	95°
3/4 teaspoon	=	3.75 milliliters	225°	105°
1 teaspoon	=	5 milliliters	250°	120°
1 tablespoon	=	15 milliliters	275°	135°
1 fluid ounce	=	30 milliliters	300°	150°
1/4 cup	=	0.06 liter	325°	165°
1/2 cup	=	0.12 liter	350°	175°
3/4 cup	=	0.18 liter	375°	190°
1 cup	=	0.24 liter	400°	205°
1 pint	=	0.48 liter	425°	220°
1 quart	=	0.95 liter	450°	230°
1 ounce weight	=	28 grams	475°	245°
1 pound	=	0.45 kilograms	500°	260°

8.31080439761